seeing the ocean through the trees

through the trees

A CONSERVATION-BASED DEVELOPMENT STRATEGY FOR CLAYOQUOT SOUND

With a Statement by Umeek

Ecotrust Canada

Nawtch-nawtch-cha [To Have a Vision]

BY UMEEK

For a long time, before the great changes took place, First Nations people had visions and consequently understood their place in the universe. It was understood that without a vision people perish, that without an understanding of place in the Creator's universe people perish, that without seeking the good powers the dark powers would prevail. These visions were understood in the heart and spirit and issued from the mouth in untold numbers of teachings.

"Hawilh, love your people." "Always be kind one to another." "Be generous." "Feed your guests." "Pay respect to those who own land and resources for they help to sustain everyone." "Take to heart and practice all the good teachings, pray with thanksgiving every day, cleanse yourself regularly, seek for good spiritual power which will contribute to the well-being of the community." "Avoid evil."

Through these visions people knew that the Creator made all things to have sacred life. Therefore all life forms were treated with respect.

Then everything changed. Newcomers came with new teachings, the chief of which might be expressed as "maximum exploitation of resources for maximum profit." Profit took precedence over people, communities, and environmental integrity. This single-minded teaching about profit has created an environmental crisis.

This crisis presents the obvious danger of continued destruction at the expense of planetary well-being, but it also presents an opportunity of creating a new vision. This new vision would do well to incorporate the best principles of ancient environmental wisdom now referred to as "traditional ecological knowledge." Ancient resource extraction strategies were guided by a profound respect for living ecosystems. Inherent in this principle is a demand for balance and harmony. Just as a genuine respect between human groups allows for a balance of power, a type of harmony between them, so too does genuine respect for living ecosystems allow for a balance of power and a type of harmony. While this kind of relationship between living entities cannot ensure life in perpetuity on planet Earth, it can ensure that life on planet Earth is not destroyed by human folly.

Contents

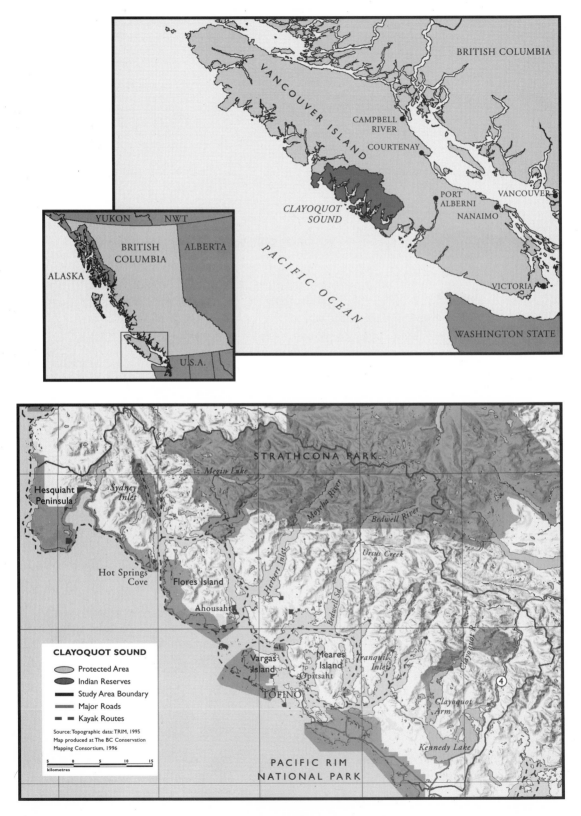

CLAYOQUOT SOUND

- Protected Area
- Indian Reserves
- Study Area Boundary
- Major Roads
- Kayak Routes

Source: Topographic data: TRIM, 1995
Map produced at The BC Conservation
Mapping Consortium, 1996

kilometres

Managing for Abundance

BY SPENCER BEEBE AND IAN GILL

The industrial age has come and gone in Clayoquot Sound, a blip on the historical
01¶ map of the rain forests of home.

The promise of prosperity and stability offered by industrial fishing and forestry sud-
denly went broke on all accounts: economic, cultural, social, and ecological. The
number and wage level of jobs declined for three decades, native culture endured a
century of denigration and decline, local communities lost their self confidence, and
02¶ the availability of salmon, herring, groundfish, shellfish and timber all plunged.

Twenty years of struggle, unprecedented civil disobedience, an incalculable amount
of local and provincial energy spent on analysis and debate—these have all been signs
of transition. The future of Clayoquot Sound—as with many other communities in
the coastal temperate rain forests of the Pacific Northwest—lies in its past. The transition taking place today is away from a narrow dependency on the forest products
industry and its cycle of resource depletion and declining employment. The shift is
back to an economy of abundance based on the richness of the sea, the tidelands, the
03¶ rivers and—to a much lesser degree—the forests.

As the focus shifts from the forests to embrace whole ecosystems, management systems must also change. In the frontier economy of the British Columbian coast,
government's role was to administer access for the exploitation of a seemingly endless
supply of natural resources. The system was autocratic, centralized, and sold to the
highest bidder. It was founded on a lazy belief that we could somehow control nature
04¶ and contain culture. The system was doomed to fail, and in Clayoquot Sound it has.

A new era in Clayoquot Sound is evolving, as it is elsewhere among communities
along North America's Pacific coast. Traditional belief systems are re-emerging,
grounded in a respect for the integrity of both nature and culture. Different systems
for restoring and allocating resources will develop to respond to the changing needs
of citizens both rural and urban. They will be more decentralized, bottom up, adap-
tive, responsive to private initiative, tolerant of diversity and respectful of natural
cycles. And they will probably bear an extraordinary resemblance to old systems—
like those of the Nuu-chah-nulth first peoples—who learned to respect the limits of
what was taken, who managed in accordance with the interconnectedness of all
05¶ things through a principle they called *hishuk ish ts'awalk*.

I

In Clayoquot Sound, the days of manipulating the region's extraordinary abundance without regard for local consequences are over. The new paradigm in Clayoquot Sound will be to manage for abundance. 06¶

In the new economy that is evolving in North America, Clayoquot Sound has an extraordinary competitive advantage of people and place. It is the only easily accessible large intact rain forest ecosystem in North America. It is blessed with the experience of five Nuu-chah-nulth First Nations, and of non-native residents whose tenacity and commitment to place have survived the hard test of a changing reality. It has to be one of the richest combinations of a productive ecosystem and diversity of people any-where in the world. It has the advantage of both proximity to cosmopolitan centres, 07¶ and sufficient distance and isolation to retain its distinctive character.

And yet its very character has been under sustained assault. Its forests have been over-harvested and its fisheries pushed dangerously towards extinction. This has been a global phenomenon, and one need only look south to Washington and Oregon to get a glimpse of what global economic trends imply for a place like Clayoquot Sound. It is a destiny the people of Clayoquot Sound—and their supporters from across Canada and around the world—have refused to accept. So in Clayoquot Sound, the machin-ery of the industrial age has been slipped out of gear. Now come the surprises. While no-one can pretend to know the directions in which the people who live in and around Clayoquot Sound will wish to go, it is clear that its communities are moving in 08¶ new directions and that individuals will need an expanding array of opportunities.

They will need more, not less, help. Not further intervention from those who pretend to know better, but enhanced access to a wider array of tools and resources than ever before; perhaps even the slight nod of encouragement all people need to employ their 09¶ own instincts and resourcefulness. There is no greater source for renewal on Earth.

This document seeks to be one such nod of encouragement. It seeks to articulate a vision that arises out of the communities of Clayoquot Sound. It attempts to give some measure of the tools available to help build that vision. Most of all, it honours the energy and ingenuity of people who understand that what is happening in 10¶ Clayoquot Sound is not an ending, but a beginning.

The Nuu-chah-nulth have a word, Ha-shilth-sa, which translates as "interesting news." It is our hope that what follows in these pages will be interesting news for the people who live in Clayoquot Sound, and for those who don't, but nonetheless rec-ognize its enormous and enduring importance. Our reporters—Katrina Kucey and David Greer—have devoted countless hours to producing an understanding of what makes Clayoquot Sound so special. They picked up the threads of what has been a long conversation about the future of Clayoquot Sound, and it is our belief that their 11¶ work will enrich that conversation.

We have attempted to stand just far enough away to both listen, and add perspective. Our hope is that, if successful, our work will result in the development of new kinds of institutions and institutional arrangements that will help concentrate the energy 12¶ already abundantly evident in Clayoquot Sound.

Reinventing Prosperity

BY IAN GILL AND DAVID GREER

On the rugged west coast of Vancouver Island, Clayoquot Sound connects several large inlets and extends for roughly 100 kilometres along the coast between Kennedy Lake and the Hesquiaht Peninsula. The Sound is renowned for the scenic beauty of its rain forests, beaches and seascapes. Fish and shellfish populations are among the highest and most diverse on the Pacific coast. The highest average annual rainfall and the mildest climate in Canada nurture the most biologically productive forest—and some of the largest trees—in the country.

For several thousand years the Nuu-chah-nulth people carefully managed the natural abundance at sea and on land by relying on their understanding of seasonal cycles to draw on a wide variety of resources without depleting them. Their relationship with the world in which they lived was shaped and supported by a belief system in which natural bounty was viewed as a gift to be treated with respect and not wasted. The refined skills and detailed knowledge needed for a prosperous way of life were passed from generation to generation through an elaborate mix of stories, songs, dances and masks inherited as family property rights. The result was one of the most sophisticated cultures in North America.

Unlike aboriginal groups in most parts of the new country, the Nuu-chah-nulth signed no treaties with Canada yet were confined to small reservations and denied access to their traditional resource base. The Europeans who displaced them viewed the natural abundance of Clayoquot Sound simply as resources to be extracted for profit. Over the course of two centuries, a succession of intensive fisheries systematically depleted sea otters, fur seals, whales, pilchards, halibut and salmon. Meanwhile, especially after a road was punched through to Clayoquot Sound in the 1950s, ancient trees were targetted for logging. Logging practices were poor, the rate of cut was unsustainable, and there was minimal economic benefit to local communities.

By the 1980s, an upwelling of opposition to the unchecked industrial exploitation of British Columbia's forests found its most ardent expression in Clayoquot Sound. Two attempts to develop a sustainable development strategy failed in the face of continued logging. In 1993, the BC government imposed its own land-use decision, protecting

3

one-third of the land area of the Sound from further development and promising 16¶ new, rigorous standards of forest management for the remainder.

To the dismay of the government, the decision was bitterly opposed. Critics said the areas protected were fragmented lands that included little rain forest, that no details of the new forest management standards had been provided, that First Nations interests had not been considered, and that no cushion had been provided for loggers who might lose their jobs. In the summer of 1993—the so-called "Clayoquot Summer"— opposition to the government's land-use decision resulted in widespread civil disobedience, more than 800 people arrested for blockading logging operations in the 17¶ Sound, and the largest mass trial in Canadian history.

Stung by the reaction, the government established an independent panel of scientists to develop new standards for sustainable forest practices. The recommendations of the Scientific Panel for Sustainable Forest Practices in Clayoquot Sound effectively brought to an end traditional industrial forestry in the Sound by recommending that ecosystem protection, rather than timber production, be the key criterion in deter- 18¶ mining future timber harvesting levels.

Meanwhile, the five First Nations of Clayoquot Sound, angered by the land-use decision's failure to acknowledge their interests in the midst of treaty negotiations, negotiated an Interim Measures Agreement with the province. The agreement secured the right of First Nations to co-manage development of their traditional territories while treaty negotiations continue. The First Nations and the BC government set up the Central Region Board, with representation from both aboriginal and non-aboriginal communities, to approve and oversee resource development. During the past two years the Central Region Board has won broad public support for its con- 19¶ sensus-based decisions.

Together, the scientific panel recommendations and Interim Measures Agreement have set the stage for a new economic framework for Clayoquot Sound—one fashioned by local communities and founded on ecosystem conservation rather than intensive resource extraction. A burst of entrepreneurial activity among local businesses in recent years provides testimony to the ability and desire of local residents to develop an economy that takes full advantage of the extraordinary diversity and 20¶ abundance of natural and scenic resources in the area.

The specific institutional steps outlined above—a land-use decision, a scientific panel, interim measures, a central planning authority—are unique to the history of Clayoquot Sound. But viewed in a regional context, what the communities of Clayoquot Sound are struggling to do is far from unique. All along the leading edge of North America, coastal communities are wrestling with how to stabilize their economies, how to conserve and restore natural ecosystems, and how to gain a mea- 21¶ sure of community control over decision-making.

"Industrial exploitation of the lands and waters of the coastal temperate rain forest has meant secure profits for a relative handful of corporate enterprises but insecure livelihoods for thousands of residents. Communities dependent on logging, mills,

1 Ecotrust, Pacific GIS and Conservation International, *The Rain Forests of Home: An Atlas of People and Place. Part 1: Natural Forests and Native Languages of the Coastal Temperate Rain Forest* (Portland, 1995), 2.

2 John C. Ryan, *State of the Northwest* (Seattle: Northwest Environment Watch, 1994), 18.

3 ShoreTrust, *The First Environmental Bancorporation®, Business Plan* (Chicago: Shorebank Corporation; Portland: Ecotrust, 1996), 14.

4 Ryan, op. cit., 15

5 Ibid, 16.

6 Ibid, 15.

7 ShoreTrust, op.cit., 14.

and coastal fisheries have seen their prosperity wax and wane with the boom-and-bust cycles typical of raw materials economies. In virtually every stretch of the eight thousand-kilometre coastline that supports these forests around the world, residents are seeking to diversify local economies and capture more of the value of raw materials 22¶ harvested and exported from the rain forest fringe."[1]

Rural communities along the forest fringe of America's Pacific Northwest and Canada's west coast represent a painful paradox. They are relatively resource rich, but increasingly impoverished and out of step with regional economic trends. The regional economy of the Pacific Northwest and BC has expanded faster than the national economies of either the United States or Canada.[2] The region "has developed a reputation for vitality that belies its boom-and-bust past."[3] On the surface, the regional economy would thus appear to be remarkably robust. The region's gross domestic product totalled $290 billion US in 1990,[4] and total personal income for the region increased five-fold (in inflation-adjusted dollars) between post-war years and the early 1990s.[5] "The Northwest generates more wealth each year than the entire 23¶ world did two centuries ago," writes John C. Ryan in State of the Northwest.[6]

But clearly such staggering gains in wealth have exacted a price. The most obvious cost has been in the depletion of natural resources, particularly timber and fish. In British Columbia, as elsewhere in the region, so strong was the belief in the abundance of those resources that little attention was paid to warning signs about their decline. In due course much of BC's natural capital was exhausted. Today, communities are paying the price, with the forest economy in disarray and the commercial 24¶ fishing industry passing from crisis to crisis.

While such losses are hard to bear, they are fairly easy to measure—in denuded hillsides, failed logging roads, choked and polluted streams, missing fish, idle mills and fishboats, frustrated workers. But something more profound has been lost that is impossible to tabulate, yet whose recovery is as vital as the return of a sockeye salmon to a natal stream. 25¶ What has been lost, and what must be recovered, is trust. That, and accountability.

People trusted that the salmon would return and they haven't. People trusted that the forests would be properly cared for and they weren't. People trusted that government and industry would act responsibly and do their jobs and they didn't. People placed their trust in systems of government and management that promised prosperity and failed to keep that promise. Yes, the regional economy as a whole is one of the strongest in the world, but that strength has masked "a significant, region-wide transition from reliance on extractive, natural-resource based industries and toward an economy guided by high technology, trade and services, with regional economic trends driven by urban-centred economic activity."[7] In other words all this newfound wealth is unevenly distributed, to the detriment of rural communities. It is in struggling coastal communities that the abuse of trust has been felt most dramatically, 26¶ and it is in those places that the work of rebuilding trust must begin.

There is no doubt that coastal communities can and will be restored to ecosystem and economic equilibrium. Ryan writes that "options long lost to most of the industrialized world still exist here. The Northwest still possesses much of its wealth of wild genes, native species, and natural processes. With this endowment we have a chance —fleeting, but still better than perhaps anywhere in the world—to rebuild tattered ecosystems and to build a durable economy…"[8]

27¶

In Clayoquot Sound, there is a better than fleeting chance to rebuild and restore a tattered ecosystem, to jealously guard what remains intact, and to build a truly durable economy. Clayoquot Sound today is the product of two economies—the traditional economy of the Nuu-chah-nulth, and the industrial economy that followed this century. Now, it is poised to enter a third economy. This new economy will respect tradition, celebrate diversity, and most of all be guided by the seasons. The ecosystem of Clayoquot Sound is dynamic, not static. So too, the new economy.

28¶

In emphasizing diversity rather than depletion, the emerging economy marks a symbolic return to the original Nuu-chah-nulth approach to management for abundance. Though they may disagree on methods, most residents of Clayoquot Sound show a common determination to support activities that retain economic value in the community while maintaining the natural values of the sound. The future prosperity of Clayoquot Sound—economic, ecological, and cultural—will depend on the ability of its people to develop a new economy that is diverse, small-scale, and conservation-based. It will be one that puts as much back into the land and sea as it takes out, and rests on a solid foundation of traditional and scientific understanding of local ecosystems and what it takes to sustain them.

29¶

With their abundance of human energy and natural wealth, the communities of Clayoquot Sound are poised to develop such an economy and set an example for other ocean-based communities along the coast. Sadly, their efforts are being frustrated. There is too much uncertainty created by institutional arrangements and policies designed for a solely industrial economy. These same policies give an empty ring to government declarations of support for local initiative. The resulting economic stagnation is wasteful and unnecessary. What is needed now is the imagination and political will to stimulate the economy of Clayoquot Sound in a way that respects natural systems and the aspirations of local people.

30¶

This means drawing on both traditional and scientific knowledge to develop an understanding of the Sound's ecosystems. Without understanding, it is not possible to determine the levels of human use that ecosystems can support.

31¶

It means changes to policy that will give those people with the greatest interest in managing resources carefully—the local communities—an opportunity to exercise that responsibility.

32¶

It means promoting economic development that overcomes long-standing institutional barriers that impede equitable access to and diverse use of the Sound's resources. In the new economy, the businesses that succeed will manage resources to restore and maintain biological diversity, will add value locally, will create less waste, use less energy, harvest no more than is replenished naturally, create local employment and improve industry standards in fishing, forestry and other fields.

33¶

---

[8] Ryan, op. cit., 65.

And it means conservation of marine areas and forested lands, either in protected areas or, as one First Nations leader in the Sound has suggested, through new desig-
34¶ nations "that don't even have names yet."

Understanding. Policy reform. Economic development. Conservation. These are the key tenets of conservation-based development, and there is perhaps no better place on the west coast to implement a conservation-based development strategy than in Clayoquot Sound. Conservation-based development is where ecology and economics intersect. It is based on the notion that economically and culturally sound communities can prosper in ways that protect the ecological integrity of their natural environment. It presumes there can be no healthy ecosystem—protected or otherwise
35¶ —unless it nurtures a healthy economy, and vice-versa.

In recent years British Columbia has shown strong leadership in promoting the principles of economic, ecological and community sustainability. Clayoquot Sound has the potential to become an example to the world of a community where those principles
36¶ are put into practice. In Clayoquot Sound, it is not too late to reinvent prosperity.

The Nuu-chah-nulth village of Ahousaht, on Flores Island. The emerging economy in Clayoquot Sound marks a symbolic return to management for abundance.

Recommendations

- Designate Clayoquot Sound as a UNESCO Man and the Biosphere Reserve.

- Redraw Clayoquot Sound's administrative boundaries to coincide with watershed boundaries, thus reflecting natural processes. Remove existing tree farm licences and fishing boundaries in favor of locally developed forestry and fishing management plans.

- Build new institutional capacity to manage all activities in Clayoquot Sound according to ecological principles and drawing on Nuu-chah-nulth traditions.

- Develop a coastal management plan that can be used as a model for local decision-making and stewardship in other coastal communities.

- Expeditiously settle Nuu-chah-nulth treaty claims.

- Establish an independent scientific body to ensure proper implementation of the recommendations of the Scientific Panel for Sustainable Forest Practices in Clayoquot Sound.

- Establish a blue-ribbon scientific panel (similar to the scientific panel on forestry) to study and make recommendations regarding the management of Clayoquot Sound's marine ecosystems and marine resource base.

- Establish an internationally funded and supported Clayoquot Centre for Coastal Studies, and build other educational capacity in the region.

- Complete a conservation strategy that protects important marine areas and the remaining pristine watersheds in Clayoquot Sound: the Sydney, Ursus, upper Bulson and Clayoquot River Valleys.

- Allow and promote community fisheries.

- Expand the woodlot program and allow local access to almost 11,000 hectares of forest lands through community forests and First Nations joint ventures that are sustainably managed and conform with ecosystem planning.

- Harvest 20,000 cubic metres of wood each year and build value-added, labor intensive wood products infrastructure around this guaranteed, sustainable wood supply.

- Create a set of community indicators for measuring socio-economic and ecosystem health over time.

- Develop a sustainable tourism strategy for Clayoquot Sound.

- Establish a permanent development institution to offer marketing, managerial and technical support, and non-bank credit to local businesses, in order to promote responsible business practices and to help grow a green market for sustainably produced goods.

- Establish "centres of excellence" for promoting "made in Clayoquot Sound" products.

The name Clayoquot derives from the name of one tribe, the Tla-o-qui-aht, or "people who are different from who they used to be." Through new institutional arrangements that better capture the opportunities for conservation-based development in Clayoquot Sound, it is possible to build a bridge over the chasm of distrust and despair that has long characterized community relations in the Sound. Only then will the promise of prosperity be kept. Then, Clayoquot Sound will become a *place* that is different from what it used to be.

Where the Forest Meets the Sea:
The Evolution of Place and People

BY DAVID GREER AND KATRINA KUCEY

The Natural History of Clayoquot Sound

Eighty kilometres west of Port Alberni, a central Vancouver Island city of lumber and paper mills, Highway 4 emerges through the mountains, winds around Kennedy Lake, and reaches a T-junction close by the open Pacific. A left turn leads to the village of Ucluelet on Barkley Sound, a right turn to the village of Tofino, at the heart of Clayoquot Sound. Between the two villages, the highway cuts across the Esowista Peninsula, where the battering waves of the Pacific have transformed glacial sediments into one of the longest and most scenic stretches of beach on the west coast of North America. Extending for almost 20 kilometres, the surf-swept sands of Long Beach and Florencia Beach each year attract several hundred thousand tourists.

Long Beach seems all the more spectacular because it stands in such marked contrast to the rocky, steeply banked coastline typical of the west coast of Vancouver Island. Rain-drenched and rugged, the coast is deeply scored with glacier-carved inlets, fed by the numerous rivers that descend from mountains in the Vancouver Island Ranges. Dense forests of red- and yellow-cedar, western hemlock, amabilis fir and Sitka spruce shoulder inlets that empty into five large Sounds, four of which take their names from the language of the original peoples of the coast. From north to south, Kyuquot, Quatsino, Nootka, Clayoquot and Barkley Sounds break up the coastline over a distance of 300 kilometres. Clayoquot Sound occupies one-third of this length and connects the series of large inlets between the Hesquiaht Peninsula and Kennedy Lake.

At the entrance to Clayoquot Sound, two large islands, Flores and Vargas, protect the inside waters from the force of the Pacific Ocean. At the centre of the Sound, the twin peaks of Meares Island loom over the fishing village of Tofino. A short paddle from the village, a grove of red-cedars on Meares contains thousand-year-old trees, including the largest known red-cedar in Canada. The "hanging-garden cedar," named for the small hemlocks, ferns and huckleberry bushes that have rooted in its ancient limbs high above the ground, is as thick as a small house is wide, and close to 20 metres in circumference as its base.

[9] R.H. Waring and J.F. Franklin, "Evergreen Forests of the Pacific Northwest," *Science* 204 (1979): 1380-86.

[10] P.A. Alaback and J. Pojar, "Vegetation from Ridgetop to Seashore," and F.L. Bunnell and A.C. Chan McLeod, "Terrestrial Invertebrates," in P. Schoonmaker, B. von Hagen, and E.C. Wolf, eds., *The Rainforests of Home: Portrait of a North American Bioregion* (Washington, DC: Island Press, 1996).

[11] C.A. Simenstad, M. Dethier, C. Levings and D. Hay, "*The Terrestrial/ Marine Ecotone,*" in P. Schoonmaker, B. von Hagen, and E.C. Wolf, eds., *The Rainforests of Home: Portrait of a North American Bioregion* (Washington, DC: Island Press, 1996).

[12] Richard E. Thompson, *Oceanography of the British Columbia Coast* (Ottawa: Department of Fisheries and Oceans, 1981), 83.

[13] "BC spot rainiest in N. America," *Vancouver Sun,* October 30, 1996, A6.

[14] Rob Butler, Canadian Wildlife Service, personal communication; Bruce Obee, "Fragile Havens for Millions of Shorebirds," *Beautiful British Columbia* (Summer, 1996), 24-29.

[15] R.E. Bilby, B.R. Fransen, and P.A. Bisson, "Incorporation of Nitrogen and Carbon from Spawning Coho Salmon into the Trophic System of Small Streams: Evidence from Stable Isotopes," *Can. J. Fish. Aquat. Sci.* 53 (1996): 164-73.

Clayoquot Sound contains the largest contiguous area of unlogged rain forest remaining on Vancouver Island, and is one of the few intact remnants of coastal temperate rain forests once found in every continent except Africa and Antarctica. Today, these once extensive forests have been virtually eliminated by settlement and industrial development. The largest remaining area of coastal temperate rain forest lies in a narrow band from western Alaska to northern California. Within this band, some of the most productive forests are found on Vancouver Island.

Coastal temperate rain forests like those of Clayoquot Sound accumulate a greater volume of organic matter per hectare than any other forest type in the world, including tropical rain forests.[9] Diversity of flora and fauna within individual stands of trees may be relatively low, but is high over the varied landscape that contains the west coast forest between the ocean shore and the mountain slopes.[10] The waters of Clayoquot Sound and in the ocean beyond are equally productive. Life activity reaches its peak in the intertidal zone, where an impressive variety of marine organisms provides food for birds and mammals of the land and ocean.[11] Offshore, the upwelling of nutrient-rich deeper waters that results when prevailing summer winds displace the warmer surface waters creates fishing yields believed to be at least a thousand times more productive than in ocean regions where upwelling is absent.[12]

The constant flow of moisture between ocean and forest ecosystems contributes hugely to their diversity and abundance. The rain forest owes its lushness both to the rain carried by the ocean winds and to the moderating climatic influence the ocean provides. In 1995 Clayoquot Lake was the wettest place in North America where measurements are recorded, with 646 centimetres (21½ feet) of rainfall.[13] Close to an inch of rain would be considered a storm of unusual intensity in many communities in North America, yet here it is the amount that falls on the forest floor, on average, every day of the year. The sheer volume of this precipitation, together with cool summers and mild winters, contributes to ideal growing conditions for the coastal rain forest, which adds nearly as much new growth in the winter as during the summer.

Aquatic life in turn is fed by the nutrients released by the intricate network of capillaries and rivulets that carries moisture from the forest floor into streams. The sediments trapped in the shallow tide flat channels in Clayoquot Sound provide ideal habitat for shellfish, crabs and the estuarine organisms that provide food for the multitude of shorebirds travelling the Pacific flyway, the migration route that winds from the southern tip of South America to the high Arctic. The Tofino mudflats attract a greater number of shorebirds than any other location on the BC coast except the Fraser delta. They also support one of the most significant populations of wintering waterbirds on the BC coast.[14] The forests of Clayoquot Sound provide nesting habitat for several species of seabird, some of which never touch land for 10 months of the year. The recent discovery that one of these seabirds, the marbled murrelet, nests in the branches of old growth trees illustrates how much is still being learned about the interdependence of species in the marine and terrestrial ecosystems.

Salmon and ancient trees symbolize the constant, symbiotic interaction between ocean and forest ecosystems. Salmon, returning from the ocean to spawn, provide

The Tofino mudflats attract shorebirds travelling the Pacific flyway.

food for the wide variety of animal and bird life that frequents the forest streams. Their carcasses provide nutrients for the riparian forests that in turn provide woody debris, a critical component of salmon habitat, to the rivers.[15] And old-growth trees likewise are as important in death as in life, providing the nurse logs that form the foundation for miniature ecosystems that in turn release nutrients to the streams and 44¶ ocean. Dead wood also adds structure to streams.

The topographical shift from the beaches and rain forest of Clayoquot Sound to the mountains to the east is dramatic. Within a few kilometres of giant coastal cedars grow delicate alpine wildflowers. Less than eight kilometres from the head of Bedwell Sound, north of Meares Island, lies the Mariner Mountain glacier, many times the size of Tofino and a final remnant of the sheets of ice that covered practically all of Vancouver Island and extended well into the Pacific until the retreat of the glaciers 45¶ between 14,000 and 12,000 years ago.

Once Were Warriors—The First Peoples of Clayoquot Sound

The ancient forests of the west coast are in fact remarkably young in geological terms. After the glaciers began to recede, the sea initially rose, then fell to a level that may have reached eleven metres below the present shoreline. Between 7,000 and 4,000 years ago, the climate became moister and cooler, and cedars began to become abundant. Later, when the first people of the coast began to develop the skills and knowledge needed ·ɔ make efficient use of the natural abundance of forest and sea, 46¶ the versatile cedar became their most valued resource in the rain forest.

Coastal temperate rain forests like those of Clayoquot Sound accumulate a greater volume of organic matter per hectare than any other forest type in the world, including tropical rain forests.

The Nuu-chah-nulth who came to occupy the entire west coast of Vancouver Island north to the Brooks Peninsula were the ancestors of about half the population of Clayoquot Sound today—the First Nations residents based in the Tla-o-qui-aht village of Opitsaht, on Meares Island; Ahousaht, on Flores Island; and Hesquiat, on Hot Springs Cove. Clayoquot Sound takes its name from the Tla-o-qui-aht people. The name is said to mean "people who are different from who they used to be." According to legend, the Tla-o-qui-aht people, once peaceful, later became fierce. Warring among First Nations groups occurred until as recently as the nineteenth century. 47¶

Before the first Europeans visited Clayoquot Sound in the late eighteenth century, the Nuu-chah-nulth peoples apparently enjoyed a stable and prosperous economy based on an intricate knowledge, developed over thousands of years, of the natural cycles of a wide variety of plant and animal species. In February, families moved into the inlets for the herring spawn. Spring was the primary time for halibut fishing and seal hunting and brought the migrations of humpback and grey whales, which the Nuu-chah-nulth hunted by canoe. In mid-summer, the focus of activity turned to salmon returning to spawn in the rivers and streams of Clayoquot Sound—first the sockeye, and later chinook and chums. Throughout the year, regardless of what other foods were available, there were shellfish close by for the taking. On land, the Nuu-chah-nulth found multiple uses for the versatile cedar: clothing from inner bark; thread from roots; planks and canoes from the trunk; even 48¶ boxes from planks steamed in pits and bent to shape.

The Nuu-chah-nulth carefully passed their detailed knowledge of species and their relationships, of hunting and gathering techniques, and of the local characteristics of land and sea from one generation to another through an elaborate system of songs, dances, masks and medicinal arts that took the form of inherited rights. Equally important in ensuring the careful management of resources was the system of property rights for land and material goods. An extended family lived in a house under the leadership of a chief who acted as custodian of resource properties such as village sites, salmon streams and ceremonial treasures. Rather than concentrating wealth, the structure of property rights was designed to ensure the sharing of resources among community members. The position of chief was more a responsibility than a privilege. This was reflected in the potlatch ceremony, in which gift-giving both

16 Grant Keddie, Curator of Archaeology, Royal British Columbia Museum, personal communication.

demonstrated the wealth and prestige of a chief and encouraged the distribution of
49¶ wealth throughout the community.

The Nuu-chah-nulth system of property rights—to land, resources, and ceremony—
evolved as a means of carefully managing for natural abundance and discouraging
wastefulness, and was founded on the understanding that, rather than dominating
nature, the Nuu-chah-nulth simply existed with and owed respect to all other creatures in the environment they inhabited. Together, belief and practice contributed to
a healthy economy that enabled the Nuu-chah-nulth to develop one of the most
sophisticated aboriginal cultures—and one of the largest aboriginal populations—in
50¶ North America.

The Coming Anarchy—Contact and Conquest

By the mid eighteenth century there were perhaps
20,000 to 50,000 Nuu-chah-nulth scattered along
the west coast of Vancouver Island, and up to
2,000 in the Clayoquot Sound area.[16] The first
contact between the Nuu-chah-nulth and
Europeans came in 1778, when Capt. James
Cook's ships came looking for the Northwest
Passage to Hudson's Bay and left with several hundred sea otter pelts. Soft, thick and silky, the sea
otter pelt rapidly became one of the most highly
prized furs in the world. The intense hunt that followed during subsequent decades left the sea otter
virtually extinct off the coast of British Columbia
by 1820. The same fate later befell the fur seal,
which was likewise hunted to near extinction by
51¶ the end of the nineteenth century.

The fact that the Nuu-chah-nulth actively assisted
the European traders in the destruction of the sea
otter and fur seal populations raises legitimate questions about how such a role could
be reconciled with their belief system. Care must be taken about over-romanticizing
the attitudes and practices of aboriginal peoples when there is no way of knowing how
their way of life might have been different with different technologies and access to
lucrative markets. Nevertheless, as a practical response to the circumstances in which
they lived, the beliefs and practices of the Nuu-chah-nulth could not have provided a
more successful means of managing their environment, and provide an instructive
counterpoint to the greed and unbridled exploitation that have too often been the
52¶ hallmark of resource management in industrial economies.

To the Europeans, resources like the sea otter and fur seal were simply commodities to
be traded for axes, blankets, metals, muskets and—as one contemporary First Nations
leader drily observes—"smallpox." The worldwide colonies that built the empires of
competing European nations were viewed as little more than storehouses of natural

MANAGING FOR ABUNDANCE IN THE NUU-CHAH-NULTH CULTURE

The belief system is the central force in defining our
culture. It is the root of all ceremony. This is seen in
the potlatch, the klu'quana, where our people give
gifts in a certain order, according to what might be
called "rank" but which is a reflection of a much more
widely ranging system.

Belief in abundance, and how to treat abundance, is at
the core. For example, before contact, there were
many times when the salmon count was down. How
we share in times of abundance with people not in
the same cycle of abundance, how to tap into other
communities experiencing abundance when you are
not—those patterns of relationships tribe to tribe are
central to who we are.

Some of the biggest changes we have experienced
have to do with a lack of access, with being denied
access to resources.

—Ron Hamilton

wealth whose exploitation was encouraged and justified through religious belief that held man to be the lord and dominator of all nature. Compared to the already depleted lands of Europe, the bounty of the north Pacific must have seemed staggering beyond belief. Traders from several nations began the process of stripping away the most valuable resources—and unwittingly provided in return the diseases that in a 53¶ matter of decades killed off the great majority of the Nuu-chah-nulth people.

The advance guard of traders was inevitably followed by the imposition of a European form of government and the appropriation of aboriginal lands after British Columbia became a Canadian province in 1871. Unlike aboriginal peoples in other parts of Canada, the Nuu-chah-nulth signed no treaties ceding their lands, yet were eventually confined to 150 small reserves totalling less than 5,000 hectares—an infinitesimal fraction of their traditional territory. In 1884 the Canadian government declared practising potlatch a criminal offence. Misconstruing the purpose of the ceremony, government officials explained that the law was intended to save the aboriginal people from impoverishing themselves. The enforced removal of aboriginal children to residential schools far from their communities, justified as being necessary for their assimilation into Canadian society, further damaged Nuu-chah-nulth culture. These children were denied the opportunity to learn from their family groups the skills they needed to gather and use the natural resources of the sea and land. Punished for speaking their own language, they no longer had access to the primary repository of 54¶ traditional knowledge. Often, they were sexually abused.

Nuu-chah-nulth woman, Clayoquot Sound. Today, the Nuu-chah-nulth comprise about half the population of the Sound.

BC Archives & Records Service. Catalogue #HP38371

The cultural impoverishment of the Nuu-chah-nulth was coupled as well with economic impoverishment. New laws denied them access to fish for food, to canoe trees, to traditional trade goods, and, through the reserve system, to their entire economic base. Involvement in non-aboriginal economic activities gradually became a matter of necessity rather than choice. Many Nuu-chah-nulth left the reserves to work in canneries and the commercial fishing and forest industries. Nuu-chah-nulth communities were hard hit by later declines in both industries. When mechanization led to a reduced workforce in the forest industry, the Nuu-chah-nulth felt the blow more severely than other communities. Most worked seasonally, in accordance with their tradition. Seasonal, non-union workers were the first to lose their jobs when industry downsized. And, when fish stocks became depleted, Nuu-chah-nulth fishers not only found themselves without jobs in the monetary economy, but also with no reserve of their traditional sea resources to 55¶ turn to.

Only in recent years have the Nuu-chah-nulth had an opportunity to restore their cultural traditions and knowledge and to start rebuilding a stable economy. The last of the residential schools was closed in the early 1970s. Many years later, adults who had lived through the humiliation imposed by the schools were still known as the "lost generation" in Nuu-chah-nulth society, with a foot in each culture and a secure place in neither. The potlatch was removed from the Criminal Code in 1951 but was rarely practised for a generation afterwards. In a society that had become so impoverished economically and in spirit, the celebration of wealth seemed strangely incongruous. In recent years, the potlatch has returned to Clayoquot Sound, and significant events once again provide opportunities for feasting, dancing, story-telling and gift-giving. The reappearance of the potlatch is a strong symbol of the restoration of Nuu-chah-nulth pride and cultural identity. But culture without land and economic opportunity is an 56¶ empty shell.

In 1980, after the Canadian government declared its willingness to negotiate treaties in BC, the Nuu-chah-nulth Tribal Council launched a land claim to traditional territories on behalf of five First Nations with traditional territory in Clayoquot Sound: the Hesquiaht, Ahousaht, Tla-o-qui-aht and two nations—the Ucluelet and Toquaht— that live at Barkley Sound but in earlier times occupied parts of Clayoquot Sound. These claims are still being negotiated between First Nations and the British Columbia and Canadian governments. In the meantime, the adult unemployment rate in Nuu-chah-nulth communities frequently hovers at around 70 per cent at a time when more than half the population in many aboriginal communities is under the age of twenty. Hence the fierce determination among Nuu-chah-nulth leaders to gain control of the tools they need to end their reliance on a narrowly focused industrial economy and to 57¶ apply their traditional expertise in broadening their economic base.

THEY USED TO LOCK ME IN THE SHOE ROOM FOR SPEAKING INDIAN

Nuu-chah-nulth management of their territorial lands and resources was shaped by their beliefs and knowledge. This knowledge was accumulated and refined over countless human generations, and was transmitted from one generation to the next through oral tradition and cultural practice. Non-verbal language included not only gestures, but also the songs, dances and masks that were passed on as family property. Through their celebration of activities such as the whale hunt or collection of herring roe, such non-verbal forms of language not only communicated essential techniques but also conveyed the respect that defined the Nuu-chah-nulth relationship with the natural world. Expertise and attitude were integrally related, in Nuu-chah-nulth belief, for hunting and gathering skills were insepa-rably linked to the skill needed to avoid waste and depletion.

When the Canadian and British Columbia governments adopted the policy of assimilating First Nations peoples into non-aboriginal society, they recognized the central role played by language. The practice of separating aboriginal children from their language in residential schools and of prohibiting the potlatch proved an effective method of undermin-ing the language of the Nuu-chah-nulth and of impoverishing their culture. Today, as the Nuu-chah-nulth work to restore their culture and to regain management of their lands and resources, the recovery of language that has so nearly been elimi-nated is a paramount concern. Renewing a depleted language is equally as important as, for example, renewing salmon stocks, for the simple reason that resources cannot be sustained over the long term without an integrated understanding of how to manage them sustainably.

The distinction between Nuu-chah-nulth beliefs about resource management and those that have until recently prevailed in non-aboriginal society is well illustrated by the vocabularies of industries. Industrial terminologies reflect and justify a belief system in which the human-nature relationship is one of domination and of domestication. It is a vocabulary of euphemisms. Timber is not logged, it is "harvested" like an agricultural crop. Forests that include dead or decaying trees are described as "decadent," implying that they have no usefulness beyond timber production, and trees with minimal timber value are labelled "weed species" and designated for destruction. The description of timber management areas as "tree farms" carries the agricultural motif to its logical conclusion: that it is the desired end of responsible forest management to convert naturally diverse ecosystems to single-crop production. Even the use of the term "resource" carries the implication that the primary purpose of nature is exploitation by humans. The borderline between unbiased communication and propaganda is a fine one. Terminology both reflects the attitudes of its creators and is instrumental in shaping the attitudes of those exposed to it.

The language spoken by the Nuu-chah-nulth is also known as Nuu-chah-nulth, and is a form of the Wakashan (Kwakiutl) language. The Nuu-chah-nulth speak two types of Wakashan (Northern and Central) and essentially four dialects. A recent survey found only nine fluent speakers and 20 lesser speakers of Nuu-chah-nulth living on the Tseshaht reserve near Port Alberni, and, in Ahousaht, 20 lesser speakers and no fluent speakers.[1] For a bioregional picture of the status of First Nations language groups, see *The Rain Forests of Home: An Atlas of People and Place* (Ecotrust, 1995).

There are currently two Nuu-chah-nulth language projects, both based at the Tseshaht reserve. The program for elementary school children emphasizes aspects of the Nuu-chah-nulth language that can be translated into English. A second program, led by elders, gathers songs and stories that emphasize traditional culture. The distinction reflects an ongoing controversy within Nuu-chah-nulth communities about the direction that should be taken in the teaching of the language. A tribal member who feels strongly that traditional knowledge should be promoted commented, "Why learn to count from 1 to 10? Why not the hidden structure in the potlatch? Language to identify and recognize the songs —the cry songs, the coming of age songs?" From this perspective, culture and language are inseparable, and to base the restoration of a language on non-aboriginal ways of thinking defeats the objective of restoring culture.

The recollections of several Nuu-chah-nulth elders who went through the residential school system provide a telling insight about the immediate and long-term consequences for children forcibly deprived of their mother tongue, and for their culture.

Edward Tatoosh: They used to lock me in the shoe room for speaking Indian. They literally went into people's homes and carted kids off to residential schools. The churches and school people thought that our dancing, our use of poles and curtains, were idolatry. Those were entitlements, and that was our history.

Kathy Robinson: I remember going up the steps, a bunch of us, and we didn't know a word of English. If we didn't know what they were saying, we got pulled by the ear. The words I remember are the ones we heard all the time—the first word I learned to say was "savage." Through that, we lost communication with our parents and grandparents. We lost communication with our brothers. In church, you couldn't turn your head to say hello to them; you had to walk right past. We lost a lot of things through that. I lost a lot of me. Things are changing, but the damage is done.

Lena Ross: A lot of parents who came from residential school didn't teach language to people like me. They didn't want us to be punished, like they were, for speaking it. It's frustrating for me to listen to an elder. I watch the way they carry themselves when they're talking. I can't understand it [the language and gestures], and it hurts.

Edward Tatoosh: I heard a nephew of mine stand up at a meeting and say, "Don't speak to me in that language. I don't know it, and you can't force me to speak it." In losing our language we lost care and concern, and we lost respect for our elders.

Lena Ross: It is a matter of changing the anger into determination. I had a lot of anger before. I am proud of what I am, and I am proud of who I am, of being Indian.

We are striving to get our language structure back, to empower people to speak in their own voice and in their own way.

---

[1] Caroline Little, personal communication.

Logging Trucks and Tourists: The Road Well Travelled

In 1959, the completion of a rough gravel road across Vancouver Island made Clayoquot Sound accessible by vehicle for the first time. Winding precariously around the sides of mountains and too narrow in some sections to accommodate vehicles from both directions, it profoundly altered the pace of life—and the pristine landscape—of 58¶ Clayoquot Sound.

Previously, the only route out was by coastal steamers such as the *Princess Maquinna*. Tofino and Ucluelet were still fishing villages, much as they had been since Scandinavian, British and Japanese settlers found their way to the west coast around the turn of the century. Only the Japanese, who had organized the local processing and packing industry, were gone—evacuated to internment camps during the Second 59¶ World War, their homes and fishboats confiscated. Few Japanese ever returned.

Fisheries were the lifeblood of the Clayoquot Sound economy for the first half of the twentieth century. The first salmon cannery opened in 1895 at Kennedy River, where large sockeye runs supported a lucrative net fishery. In the 1920s, a pilchard fishery developed to capitalize on the massive runs of these sardine-like fish, valued for their oil. Among the 26 pilchard-reduction facilities that sprang up along the west coast of Vancouver Island were six in Clayoquot Sound. By the mid-1940s the pilchards had vanished entirely, never to return, and many of the seiners that had netted them moved to the herring fishery. Other seiners fished the halibut banks off the coast until halibut stocks became depleted in the mid-1950s. Throughout this period, the seine fishery was complemented by the growth of an expanded trolling fleet. Prior to the 1960s, troll-caught salmon were packed in ice and shipped to Vancouver by boat for the fresh market. The road from Alberni, rough as it was, introduced trucking services to the coast. Within a few years, salmon from Clayoquot Sound were being 60¶ trucked out, and the packers gradually disappeared.

Ucluelet, in addition to its fishing fleet, supported a community of loggers, many of whom worked at small logging operations like the one that started up at Kennedy Lake in the late 1940s. Clayoquot Sound was simply too inaccessible and too far from timber markets to make the transportation of log booms through the treacherous west-coast waters economical. For several decades, Vancouver Island timber was obtained primarily from the thick Douglas fir forests of the Esquimalt and Nanaimo Railway land grant on the east coast of Vancouver Island. As these forests became depleted, and as truck logging began to replace railway logging in the 1950s, a web of rough roads started to spread west into the mountains, opening access to the massive timber on the west coast. The road to the coast was built by forest companies as a condition of their tree farm licences—a new form of area-based timber tenure that had been created in part to put an end to "cut-and-run" logging by companies with long-term tenure and therefore no stake in sustaining a healthy forest. Through tree farm licences, BC Forest Products and MacMillan Bloedel obtained the rights to a large majority of the publicly 61¶ owned forest land in Clayoquot Sound during the 1950s.

In addition to opening up the coast to industrial logging, the new road incidentally provided the way in for tourists. The mystique of Long Beach, remote and unspoiled, was enhanced by tales of the hair-raising road to the west coast. Passengers of cars forced to the edge by oncoming traffic described the sight of wrecks in the chasm below the cliff edge—reminders of less successful journeys. In the late 1960s, in response to public pressure to protect Long Beach, the federal government announced its intention to create a national park. Outdoor recreation enthusiasts coalesced into a lobby group demanding inclusion in the park of the Nitinat Triangle, a series of lakes in an unlogged watershed south of Barkley Sound. The eventual success of their efforts acted as a springboard for the growth of groups dedicated to the protection of other unspoiled environments on Vancouver Island. 62¶

Many summer visitors to Long Beach took up permanent residence in the Tofino area. In 1972, the paving of Highway 4 made the laborious trip over nerve-wracking switchbacks a thing of the past. As the flow of tourists continued to swell, the development of restaurants, resorts and other services gradually began to change the character of the fishing village. Ucluelet, meanwhile, became home to a growing population of forestry workers as logging activity expanded on the west coast of Vancouver Island. The two villages, which had both grown around the fishing industry, were beginning to take on distinctly different characteristics—and attitudes. 63¶

The creation of a national park at Long Beach in 1971 was a springboard for the growth of groups dedicated to protecting other unspoiled areas on Vancouver Island.

Deciding the Fate of the Rain Forest: Conflict and Compromise

BY DAVID GREER AND KATRINA KUCEY

During the 1960s and 1970s, the appetite of forestry companies for virgin timber grew rapidly in response to market demands and the development of sophisticated harvesting technologies. As the patchwork of clearcut openings across Vancouver Island grew, parts of Highway 4 to the coast revealed to tourists a burned-out, denuded wasteland advancing ever closer to the pristine slopes of Clayoquot Sound.

MacMillan Bloedel's announcement in 1980 that it intended to log parts of Meares Island, Clayoquot Sound's best-known landmark, set off a storm of protest in nearby communities. Nuu-chah-nulth leaders condemned the planned desecration of an island that had tremendous spiritual significance to their people. Tofino town council protested to the Ministry of Forests that visible logging on Meares would degrade its water supply, hurt the emerging tourist industry, and lower property values. Oyster farmers expressed concern about the potential impact of water pollution on their leases. The Friends of Clayoquot Sound, an organization dedicated to the preservation of the area's rain forest, condemned the threat to the old-growth ecosystem. Thus began a conflict that, like Meares itself, would become a focal point of life in Clayoquot Sound for more than a decade.

An attempt to resolve the dispute through an impromptu multi-party process was aborted when MacMillan Bloedel withdrew and presented its own plan to the provincial cabinet, which approved the company's proposal. Angry residents responded by launching boat blockades against MacMillan Bloedel's attempts to set up logging operations. Their nerve attracted widespread attention throughout British Columbia. Elsewhere, challenges to the entrenched rights of forest companies had been relatively polite and ineffective.

As expected, MacMillan Bloedel applied for and was granted a court injunction against the blockaders. There the matter might have ended, had not the Nuu-chah-nulth nations, which had just launched a land claim to their traditional territories, taken a page from the forest company's book by applying for their own court injunction against timber harvesting on Meares Island. In a landmark decision in 1985, the

A web of roads begun in the 1950s opened up the west coast to truck logging, fuelling the dramatic over-cutting of Clayoquot Sound's forests.

BC Court of Appeal approved the application pending the outcome of treaty negotiations—a 67¶ process likely to last many years.

The Meares Island decision provided inspiration to many people who were feeling increasingly hopeless about holding back the tide of industrial development in Clayoquot Sound. A focus for further action was provided in 1987 by the report of the United Nations-sponsored World Commission on Environment and Development, which expressed grave concern about the impact of industrial excesses on the environment and called on all nations to promote "development that meets the needs of the present without compromising the ability of future generations to meet their own needs."[17] "Sustainable develop- ment" quickly became a rallying cry for environ- 68¶ mental groups.

A year later, after 35 people were arrested at a blockade of a forest access road at Sulphur Pass, north of Flores Island, the Tofino-Long Beach Chamber of Commerce and the Tofino District Council called on the BC government to approve their proposal for the preparation of a sustainable development strategy for Clayoquot Sound.[18] On a visit to the area, Premier Bill Vander Zalm expressed dismay at the extent of clearcutting operations. Shortly afterwards, cabinet announced the creation of the Clayoquot Sound Sustainable Development Task Force, to be chaired by a professional mediator and charged with negotiating consensus on a sustainable development strategy. The process ground on for a year before collapsing in disagree- 69¶ ment about interim logging plans and about who had the right to be at the table.

In January 1991, faced with the prospect of escalating conflict, the government made a second attempt, establishing a Clayoquot Sound Sustainable Development Steering Committee with an expanded membership. It too faltered, after environmentalists denounced what they saw as a strategy to "talk and log" and walked away from the process. Then, after a provincial election largely won on a promise to end the "forest wars" that were raging through the province, the New Democratic Party government set up the independent Commission on Resources and Environment (CORE) to oversee the development of a province-wide land use strategy that would meet the new government's commitment to implement sustainable forest practices and double the 70¶ area protected from development to 12 from 6 per cent of the provincial land base.

Cabinet instructed CORE to develop a comprehensive land use plan for Vancouver Island, but excluded Clayoquot Sound from CORE's deliberations, ostensibly because a consensus-based process was already underway in the area. The decision infuriated the environmental groups that had walked out of the process. In the end, hampered by the absence of clear criteria for the selection of protected areas and of a

[17] World Commission on Environment and Development, *Our Common Future* (Oxford: Oxford University Press, 1987), 8.

[18] Craig Darling, *In Search of Consensus: An Evaluation of the Clayoquot Sound Sustainable Development Task Force* (Victoria: UVic Institute for Dispute Resolution, 1991), 10.

The long, hot summer of 1993. More than 800 people were arrested for objecting to a flawed plan resulting from a failed process. Photo: Bo Myers

government strategy for dealing with displaced forest workers, the steering committee could not agree on the future of several intact watersheds and on appropriate methods of timber harvesting. The committee co-chairs suggested to government that it protect those areas agreed upon by all members of the committee and refer the rest to CORE. But the multi-party negotiations on a land use plan for Vancouver Island were already looking precarious. The addition of Clayoquot Sound, which by now was drawing national attention as Canada's most notorious environmental "hot spot," had the potential to derail not only the Vancouver Island process but other regional negotiations throughout the province. Declining the advice from the co-chairs, cabinet gambled on drawing a new map for the Sound and winning enough public 71¶ support to make it fly.

The Year of Living Dangerously—The 1993 Land Use Decision

The government's land use decision, made public in April 1993, divided Clayoquot Sound into three zones: protected, integrated resource management, and special management. To the existing 39,000 hectares in protected areas in the Sound (primarily Pacific Rim National Park and the western portion of Strathcona park) were 72¶ added another 48,500 hectares.

In total, approximately one-third of the land area in the Sound was protected after the decision. The remainder of the land was designated for integrated resource management for a variety of economic activities, among which timber harvesting would

21

continue to predominate. Approximately one-quarter of the integrated resource management area was designated a special management zone in which development plans would be required to take into account recreational, wildlife and scenic values.

The government estimated that the decision would result in a reduction in the annual cut from 900,000 to 600,000 cubic metres. New protected areas accounted for two-thirds of this reduction. The remainder would result from the protection of scenic and wildlife values and from the implementation of new, world-leading timber harvesting practices and standards. It was estimated that the decision would result in the loss of 400 direct forestry jobs.[19]

To balance the inevitable criticism of the decision from industry and unions, the government counted on broad public support for increased protection of the rain forest. It noted that the decision not only more than doubled the amount of protected area but would protect biodiversity by creating a large natural reserve of temperate old-growth forest to link the interior mountains to the ocean shore. The adjacent Megin and Upper Shelter Inlet watersheds made up slightly more than half of the new protected area. For the most part, the remainder was made up of a scattering of lands at Sydney Inlet, the Hesquiaht Peninsula, Flores and Vargas islands, Clayoquot Arm and Clayoquot Plateau.

In reality, other than in a single large watershed, the Megin, the new protected areas were largely made up of unproductive fragments of land with limited value for timber extraction. The remaining unlogged watersheds—the most productive lands—remained entirely or partially open to harvesting. Moreover, the decision provided

[19] Government of British Columbia, "Clayoquot Sound Land Use Decision: Background Report" (Victoria, 1993), passim.

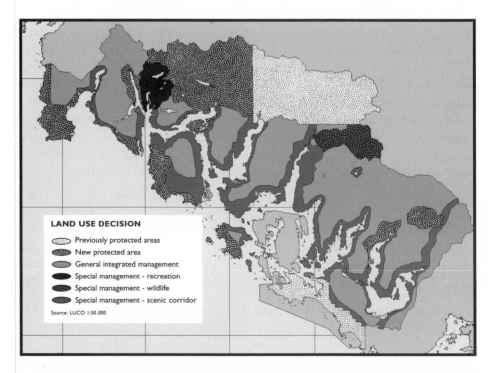

LAND USE DECISION
- Previously protected areas
- New protected area
- General integrated management
- Special management - recreation
- Special management - wildlife
- Special management - scenic corridor

Source: LUCO 1:50,000

virtually no protection of contiguous old-growth and marine ecosystems, or of the shores of sheltered marine areas and estuaries. Finally, unlike CORE's later proposal for the Vancouver Island Land Use Plan, which emphasized the need for biological connectivity through undeveloped corridors linking protected areas, protected areas in Clayoquot Sound largely consisted of widely separated patches of land surrounded by areas open to industrial activity.

76¶

The land use decision fell squarely in an established tradition in which governments make unpopular decisions by compromise, hold tight, and weather out the predicted storm of criticism. In Clayoquot Sound, however, both the stakes and expectations of local residents had become too high over the years for such a strategy to work. The forest industry and unions condemned the decision not only for the reduction in timber supply and loss of jobs, but for including no clear strategy for dealing with several hundred displaced workers. The environmental movement decried the continued logging of one of the most magnificent examples of coastal temperate rain forest remaining in the world. And the Nuu-chah-nulth criticized a failure to consult them over the allocation of their traditional lands for parks and logging. The Friends of Clayoquot Sound rallied support against the decision across the country and internationally, painting a picture of the last of the rain forests being pulped for telephone directories in Europe and the US. In the summer of 1993, several thousand people visited the "Peace Camp" established in a clearcut near an access road to current logging operations. The blockades that followed led to the arrest of more than 800 people and the largest mass trial in Canadian history.

77¶

Like the ancestors of the Tla-o-qui-aht tribe, the residents of Clayoquot Sound were people different from what they used to be. Years of pitched battles over logging in the Sound had bred a new generation of warriors, native and non-native. Many people who travelled to the Sound to participate in the blockade of a logging road saw the dispute in terms of protecting from the chainsaw one of the last and most extensive remnants of the world's remaining coastal temperate rain forests. But for local residents, timber harvesting was part and parcel of a broader concern that ran through all Clayoquot Sound communities.

78¶

BEING THERE—THE CLAYOQUOT BIOSPHERE PROJECT
By David Greer

Land use planning processes in Clayoquot Sound, as elsewhere in British Columbia, historically have suffered from a lack of reliable and comprehensive information about ecosystem characteristics and species relationships. Until recent years, the collection and analysis of such information has received low priority, and the little information that was gathered tended to be narrowly focused on the few species considered important—for example, the

impact of logging on ungulates. Planning is only as good as the information on which it is based. The results of poorly informed planning processes—most notably in forestry and commercial fishing—have been devastating to the integrity of coastal temperate rain forest ecosystems.

The Clayoquot Biosphere Project—a community-based, non-profit research and education society—was set up in 1991 to start building information about the natural biodiversity and ecological processes of the temperate coastal ecosystem. In part, the Biosphere Project was inspired by the intimate knowledge among many Nuu-chah-nulth people of local ecosystems—knowledge that did not exist in the scientific community and included an understanding of natural variations in species abundance and distribution, habitat and food require- ments, behaviour patterns, ecology, and physiology.

The organizers of the Biosphere Project concluded that the first step to finding out about intact ecosystems was to be there for extended periods. This not only allows a careful description of the place (through biological inventories) but makes possible the equally important study of the dynamics in an ecosystem over time, by documenting the subtle effects of changing weather conditions, the movements and interactions of animal species, and the life cycles of plant species. Initially, the basic questions to be answered were: what species are present and when, and which areas are important to them and why? To facilitate observation and study, the Biosphere Project has built research stations at three remote locations at Clayoquot Lake (1992), the west coast of Flores Island (1994), and the Sydney River estuary (1996). Respectively, these three stations enable the study of an intact rain forest ecosystem, a marine ecosystem, and, through a study of estuary life, the interaction between forest and ocean.

The cabin at the Clayoquot station has been used for more than 250 days each year since its inception, with trained volunteers making detailed natural history observations that provide invaluable information on natural ecosystems and natural events such as rain—the driving force that governs so much activity, from water temperature, to salmon movements, to the movements of salmon predators, to the massive shifting of stream debris. A permanent vegetation plot allows researchers to determine the changes in forest vegetation over time; measure biomass, leaf area, snags and logs, timber volume, and the relation of forests to wildlife species; and compare global relationships between climate, soils and disturbances to forest structure and composition. Complementing human observation, computerized environmental monitoring stations provide hourly readings for temperature, sunlight, humidity, rainfall, lake or ocean temperature and depth.

The initial studies at the Clayoquot research station have provided several basic insights that will allow better questions to be posed to further a greater understanding of the ecosystem. For instance, it has become clear that calendar years have little mean-

ing for an understanding of cycles of wildlife activity, where there may be intervals of two or three years between visits of cougars and bears. Similarly, studying a single watershed has limited usefulness in understanding the behaviour patterns of wildlife that range to adjacent or more distant watersheds. Moreover, a single watershed such as the Clayoquot Valley contains within it many different biological components and communities. It is wrong to assume that protecting one area provides an adequate "representative" sample of a larger ecosystem. What this makes clear is that the definition of "ecological integrity" customarily used in planning processes—maintaining populations of "important" species or maintaining representative examples of intact landscapes—can no longer suffice. Far more important is the maintenance of a full spectrum of natural species and processes.

The work in the Clayoquot River valley has provided an excellent model for studies being conducted at the two more recently established research stations. On the coast of Flores Island, where a underwater plot has been marked out for detailed observation of seabed life, research is focusing on gray whale feeding ecology, basking shark behaviour and abundance, intertidal foraging behaviour of bears, and subtidal inventories. At the Sydney estuary station, studies are beginning on the interactions between land and sea.

The work of the Biosphere Project has sparked widespread interest among the international scientific community and has provided the material for numerous reports that have contributed to the building of knowledge about coastal ecosystems. Its success has been due to the collective efforts of professional biologists, students, and volunteers. The next step is to expand the Biosphere Project into a Clayoquot Centre for Coastal Studies, which will forge closer links with academic institutions and increase the organization's capacity as a community-based research facility with a network of field stations, classrooms, and a laboratory. By continuing to build scientific understanding and expertise among local residents, both aboriginal and non-aboriginal, the Clayoquot Centre for Coastal Studies will enable the communities of Clayoquot Sound to participate far more effectively in planning processes, to be recognized for their local expertise, and to provide the solid base of ecological information needed to make those processes credible.

The control of over 90 per cent of the public land in Clayoquot Sound by two international forest companies was a constant reminder of the obstacles to local communities having a meaningful say in their own destiny. It wasn't just about distribution of wealth. It was about people being told to simply accept the broad swaths in the landscape left by clearcuts. It was about landslides and streamside logging that destroyed the spawning habitat of the salmon that sustained local economies. Residents who collected or farmed shellfish and crabs not only had to contend with

In essence, the scientific panel concluded that the critics of BC forest practices had been right all along.

the effects of silt and other pollution, but even required permission from the forest companies to obtain the foreshore lease they needed to make a living. At a time when communities were anxious to take advantage of opportunities to diversify their economy in an ecologically sound manner, the current system of forest management

79¶ symbolized all the impediments that blocked their way.

Co-managing Clayoquot: The Interim Measures Agreement and the Central Region Board

In March 1994, after a report by the BC Ombudsman office criticized the BC government for failing to consult adequately with First Nations in the Clayoquot Sound land-use decision, the province concluded an agreement with the hereditary chiefs of the five Nuu-chah-nulth nations with an interest in Clayoquot Sound. The Interim Measures Agreement (IMA), so-called because it relates to matters on the table in the treaty negotiation process, provides for a degree of joint management of lands and

80¶ resources in Clayoquot Sound.

The IMA set up the Ahousaht-Tla-o-qui-aht Cooperative Forest Management Area on Flores Island and in the Clayoquot River valley, with provincial financial assistance for forest management in the area. On the Hesquiaht Peninsula, defined as an economic development base for the Hesquiaht First Nation, the IMA provided that all new development would take into account the Management for a Living Hesquiaht Harbour plan and incorporate First Nations interests. To the south of Clayoquot Sound, a secure position for the Toquaht in the forest industry was to be established in their traditional territory. Finally, a joint working group was established to promote First Nations economic development opportunities in a variety of enterprises, including forestry, stream rehabilitation, salmon enhancement, road reclamation, silviculture, trail construction, park management, tourism, skills train-

81¶ ing, shellfish harvesting, and whale-watching tours.

The IMA also set up a new body for joint governance in land use and resource management matters. With membership to be jointly appointed by the First Nations and the province, the Central Region Board (CRB) was given a broad mandate regarding all future land and resource management decisions, including logging, reforestation, mining, road-building, aquaculture, wildlife management, recreation and parks. This includes authority to recommend amendments or rejection of plans and to refer unresolved recommendations to the provincial cabinet, which retains legislated decision-making authority. However, the IMA provided for a further step in the event that cabinet should fail to accept a CRB recommendation. In that case, the matter would be referred to a newly created Central Region Resource Council, made up of hereditary chiefs and cabinet ministers, which would publicly attempt to resolve the issues at the political level. 82¶

The ultimate objective of the CRB's activity was to be the promotion of economic and environmental sustainability of both aboriginal and non-aboriginal communities throughout the Clayoquot Sound region. This balance of aboriginal and non-aboriginal needs was reflected in the decision-making process defined for the CRB. In the absence of consensus, board decisions would require a double majority of First Nations and provincial representatives.[20] On the renegotiation of the Interim Measures Agreement in 1996, provision was made for all meetings of the board to be open to the public except where the co-chairs direct that certain meetings be held in private.[21] The CRB currently comprises 10 members. Each of the five First Nations appoints one representative, and there are five provincial appointees, including one each nominated by Tofino, Ucluelet and the Regional District of Alberni-Clayoquot. Port Alberni was invited to nominate a representative but declined, indicating that its 83¶ interests would be represented through the regional district.

The Central Region Board has gained wide respect and acceptance among residents as the central decision-making body in Clayoquot Sound. In contrast to earlier decision-making processes in the Sound, the CRB has an enviable record of success in achieving consensus on issues placed before it. The fact that it is perceived as being truly representative of the interests of local communities, rather than being constrained by the 84¶ priorities of government and industry, has earned it enormous credibility.

A decade ago, the Nuu-chah-nulth were virtually excluded from major land and resource management decisions. Indeed, their application for an injunction against clearcut logging of Meares Island, the home of the Tla-o-qui-aht people and a place of tremendous spiritual significance, was regarded at the time as a futile gesture of defiance of a management system that customarily, and with legal sanction, largely ignored First Nations interests. Given that recent history, the recognition of Nuu-chah-nulth authority in the Interim Measures Agreement signalled a major change in the relationship between aboriginal and non-aboriginal peoples in Clayoquot Sound, and held out the promise that consensus would at last replace conflict in resolving 85¶ land use issues in Clayoquot Sound.

Today, through such projects as Management for a Living Hesquiaht Harbour, and Geographic Information Systems (GIS) mapping on Flores Island, the Nuu-chah-nulth are building on their traditional knowledge to develop the inventories that will form the foundation for the management of their land and ocean resources. Through initiatives such as the salmon hatchery operated by the Tla-o-qui-aht First Nations on the Clayoquot River, and steps towards the restoration of sockeye habitat being undertaken by the Kennedy Lake Technical Working Group, they are working to

[20] "Interim Measures Agreement between Her Majesty the Queen in Right of the Province of British Columbia and the Hawiih of the Tla-o-qui-aht First Nations, the Ahousaht First Nation, the Hesquiaht First Nation, the Toquaht First Nation and the Ucluelet First Nation," 19 March 1994.

[21] "Clayoquot Sound Interim Measures Extension Agreement," 24 April 1996.

[22] "Commission on Resources and Environment, "Public Report and Recommendations Re Issues Arising from the Government's Clayoquot Sound Land Use Decision," 22 April 1993, 3.

[23] "The Government of British Columbia's Response to the Commission on Resources and Environment's Public Report and Recommendations Regarding Issues Arising from the Clayoquot Land Use Decision," 1 June 1993.

restore depleted salmon stocks. Other steps to rebuild aboriginal economies include tourism-related initiatives such as whale-watching tours and the Wild Side Heritage Trail on Flores Island.

86¶

The Kennedy Lake Technical Working Group and the West Coast Sustainability Association are examples of current initiatives where Nuu-Chah-Nulth and non-aboriginal residents of Clayoquot Sound are working together to promote more stable economic and ecological conditions in Clayoquot Sound. One of the important challenges of the future will be to develop other informal avenues of cooperation that supplement joint management protocols and create opportunities for aboriginal and non-aboriginal communities alike.

87¶

The Quest for Understanding—The Scientific Panel

Even before the Central Region Board was brought into being, the government was brought to account regarding another of its promises in the 1993 land-use decision. Within days of the 1993 decision, CORE called on the government to provide details of the stringent forest management practices and standards promised in the decision, pointing out the need to assure a skeptical public that there was substance to the commitment.[22] In response, the government offered to establish, in cooperation with CORE, an independent, blue ribbon scientific panel to review standards and make recommendations for changes and improvements.[23] The Scientific Panel for Sustainable Forest Practices in Clayoquot Sound included scientists expert in regional ecology and biodiversity; engineers and foresters experienced in forestry planning, management and engineering; earth scientists with expertise in soils, slope stability and hydrology; fisheries and wildlife biologists; a scenic resources, recreation and tourism planner; and an ethnobotanist. Traditional aboriginal knowledge, which had previously been largely ignored in land and resource management, was presented through the membership of a chief and three elders from the Nuu-chah-nulth Central Region tribes. This was a major and long overdue recognition that aboriginal and local ecological knowledge play a fundamental role in anchoring science, rooting it in a place.

88¶

The scientific panel began by developing a set of general and guiding principles based on the premise that timber harvesting cannot be sustained over the long term unless forest ecosystems are understood and sustained—a conclusion that had been reached in one form or another by a succession of forest resources commissions for 80 years but had never been effectively addressed. It logically followed that planning should focus on what was retained in the forest rather than what was removed, and should be based on natural ecosystem boundaries—those of watersheds—rather than fragmenting ecosystems. Moreover, planning should draw not only on currently limited scientific understanding but also on the traditional, detailed knowledge developed by aboriginal peoples over several thousand years.

89¶

The scientific panel found that the existing approach to forest management did not come close to meeting its guiding principles. The status quo did not adequately recognize First Nations values and perspectives, was inadequate for sustainable ecosystem management, and was insufficient for the protection of undeveloped watersheds in Clayoquot Sound. In keeping with its emphasis on the integrity of ecosystems, the panel recommended that conventional clearcutting methods in Clayoquot Sound be replaced with the adoption of a variable-retention silvicultural system that would ensure maintenance of natural age and class distributions of trees, and that yarding, log-handling and road-building methods be altered to minimize their impact on ecosystems.[24] In essence, the panel concluded that the critics of BC forest practices had been right all along.

90¶

SCIENTIFIC PANEL GENERAL PRINCIPLES

1 The world is interconnected at all levels; attempts to understand it entail analysing its components and considering the whole system.
2 Human activities must respect the land, the sea, and all the life and life systems they support.
3 Long-term ecological and economic sustainability are essential to long-term harmony.
4 The cultural, spiritual, social and economic well-being of indigenous people is a necessary part of that harmony.
5 Restoration of historical degradation is a necessary part of a healthy human relationship with the land.
6 Standards must accommodate new information and changing social values.
7 Information on the resources of Clayoquot Sound and understanding of its forest ecosystems are incomplete.
8 Standards cannot be designed to meet all situations that will be encountered on the ground.
9 British Columbia can and should show leadership in the stewardship of forest ecosystems.[25]

In the eighteen months of its existence, the scientific panel produced an extraordinary body of detailed analysis and recommendations. This was the first time in the history of the province that resource management practices had been so meticulously analysed with a primary view to ecosystem integrity and long-term social and economic needs. In July 1995, the provincial government adopted the scientific panel's more than 120 recommendations in their entirety.

91¶

Although the scientific panel had no authority to recommend changes to the Clayoquot Sound land use decision, its findings ultimately shaped the future of the rain forests far more than did the lines on the map created by the 1993 land use decision. By giving definition to the higher forest practice standards promised by the government, the panel had a greater impact on timber supply than did the doubling of protected areas. By setting ecosystem sustainability rather than timber sustainability as the fundamental criterion for the determination of timber supply, the scientific panel effectively rendered obsolete the allowable annual cut that had for decades guided logging on tree farm licences. The government's prediction of an annual cut of 600,000 cubic metres under the land use decision no longer held meaning.

92¶

Even while accepting the panel's recommendations in full—by then a matter of political necessity—the government had only a limited appreciation of what the impact of those recommendations might be. Many forest workers have grudgingly come to accept that the scientific panel's principles make sense, but there is ongoing uncertainty about the precise meaning of the panel's recommendations and the long-term effect of their implementation on timber supplies and forestry-related employment. Environmentalists have criticized the fact that the panel was constrained from recommending any changes to the land-use plan that would protect more areas, especially the pristine watersheds. But with that caveat, they have mostly accepted that the scientific panel's recommendations will guide future forest development in the Sound. First Nations have agreed to support the recommendations, and industry has promised to work with government and First Nations to implement them.

93¶

[24] Scientific Panel for Sustainable Forest Practices in Clayoquot Sound, *Report 5: Sustainable Ecosystem Management in Clayoquot Sound: Planning and Practices* (April 1995), passim.

[25] Scientific Panel for Sustainable Forest Practices in Clayoquot Sound, *Report 1* (January 1994), 6.

The Lay of the Landscape:
Mapping the Scientific Panel Recommendations

BY DAVID CARRUTHERS, EDWARD BACKUS,
MIKE MERTENS, LISA LACKEY

The recommendations of the Scientific Panel for Sustainable Forestry Practices in Clayoquot Sound have enormous implications for the future of the forest industry in the region. A government-led process has been established to implement the stringent forest management standards recommended by the panel. And in response to the panel's concerns about lack of adequate information about forest ecosystems and resource values, government and industry are engaged in ecosystem mapping and development of inventories. To date, however, no calculation has been made of the ultimate effect that implementing the panel's recommendations will have on the volume of timber that can be removed from the forests of Clayoquot Sound.

Ecotrust Canada, in collaboration with the BC Conservation Mapping Consortium, has undertaken its own landscape analysis of the scientific panel's recommendations. This analysis decisively demonstrates that industrial forestry no longer has a place in Clayoquot Sound. Using scientific panel criteria, our analysis shows that, if faithfully implemented, the panel's guidelines effectively constrain logging on all but a small area of forested land in the Sound. The following series of maps, produced on a Geographic Information System, provides compelling evidence that only the most limited amount of timber extraction can be sustained if Clayoquot Sound is to be developed according to the "world-class standards" promised by the provincial government. Our analysis should not be seen as cause for alarm. Far from signalling an end to prosperity, it announces the beginning of a new economy based on ecosystem and community health.

The scientific panel calls for ecosystem sustainability rather than timber supply to be the key governing criterion for forest management in the Sound. In order to achieve this, the panel recommends that at the watershed level, maps should be made which designate reserves of sensitive areas where no harvesting should occur. The idea here is that, once highly valued and sensitive areas are set aside, cut-block plans can then be developed on what is left over. The maps presented in Chapter 4 should be viewed as a progression—a set of filters which build to a final constraints map.

As maps 1-9 show on pages 36-53, implementing the scientific panel recommendations will leave little place for traditional industrial forestry in Clayoquot Sound. In fact, the amount of land that can actually be logged in the Sound amounts to 22,916.31 hectares if the scientific panel's rules are followed. 97¶

Map 10 takes the analysis one step further than the scientific panel's recommendations by demonstrating the effect of not allowing logging in the remaining pristine watersheds in Clayoquot Sound. Despite the widespread acceptance of the scientific panel's recommendations, it has been criticized for its failure to address the fate of pristine areas. 98¶

The amount of land in the scientific panel's study area—that is, all Clayoquot Sound with the exception of the town of Tofino, and Meares Island—totals 254,726.04 hectares. Of that area, 138,672.38 hectares, or 54.4 per cent, are considered pristine (a watershed is judged to be pristine if it is less than 2 per cent developed). Of the pristine watersheds, 71,451.83 hectares are already protected. That means 67,220.55 99¶ hectares of pristine watersheds remain unprotected in Clayoquot Sound.

The scientific panel's rules, however, effectively constrain logging in the Sound, as mentioned above, to an area totalling 22,916.31 hectares. Most, but not all of the pristine watersheds are thus de facto protected by the "world-class standards" promised by the provincial goverment and prescribed by the scientific panel. Taking the scientific panel's work one step further and explicitly constraining any future logging in pristine watersheds—the difference, in other words, between Map 9 and Map 10—means that the fate of just 12,132.48 hectares of land, or a mere 4.76 per cent of all Clayoquot Sound, is all that stands in the way of completing the protection of the Sound's superb pristine watersheds for all time. Put another way, an agreement to protect all the remaining unprotected pristine watersheds in Clayoquot Sound, totalling 67,220.55 hectares, really only involves a net removal from the area open to 100¶ logging of just over 12,000 hectares of land.

The effect of doing so would be to leave a total area of 10,784.38 hectares open to logging in Clayoquot Sound. That is, there can be total protection of the remaining pristine watersheds, and the scientific panel's recommendations can be applied throughout the Sound, and nearly 11,000 hectares of land can be safely opened up to logging to world-class standards. According to available forest cover data, the land in question would yield a total of 100,700.76 cubic metres of wood over five years, or 20,140.15 cubic metres per year. Clearly, this is not sufficient to support an industrial forestry base that used to routinely take 40 times that amount of timber from Clayoquot Sound every year, a rate of cut which has since been shown to have been utterly unsustainable. It is also significantly less than the 900,000 cubic metres over five years being demanded by the International Woodworkers of America-Canada, which claims that 80 union jobs are in peril in the region if 180,000 cubic metres per 101¶ year is not cut.[26]

But according to the provincial government's own figures, 1.34 jobs are created for every 1,000 cubic metres cut according to standard logging practices.[27] So at the very least, the 20,140.15 cubic metres per year that is available to be logged sustainably can

[26]"Loggers dispute MacBlo Figures," *Times Colonist,* Victoria, 15 January, 1997.

[27]"Arrowsmith TSA Socio-Economic Analysis," Alan Fitzgibbon and Associates, for Economic and Trade Branch, Ministry of Forests (August 1995), 39.

Roman Frank of the Ahousaht GIS department.
"We will help to make a difference for our children."

BRIDGING THE GAP
By Roman Frank

Since the Ahousaht Geographic Information Systems program began in early 1995, we have been guided by the following mission:

> *We are here in order to capture the essence of our elders' history. Our duties will be to bridge the gap of knowledge between these elders and our next generation of Ahousaht members. In bridging this gap, we hope to ensure the existence of our peoples for years to come.*

Our secondary duties will be to apply this knowledge effectively in managing our own resources. By combining both historical wisdom with our technical knowledge, we will give our leaders a much greater opportunity to succeed.

At the outset of our program, much time was spent learning how to operate the software modules, and how to conduct the day-to-day business of a GIS. In September of 1995, we received a copy of PC ARC/INFO 3.4.2 for our office. Afterwards our training took on an entirely new aspect. We began looking at data creation, manipulation, and data output at a much higher scale than previously had been achievable. With the aid of Interrain Pacific and the BC Conservation Mapping Consortium, we trained with basic GIS processing exercises such as input, analysis and output (through ArcView 2.0).

A critical step for us was gaining acceptance of our program by our own band council. Much work remains to be done locally to educate our people about the full potential of the GIS. Our biggest obstacle is the challenge presented by changing from a rigidly oral history to our system of technological wizardry. Many of our elders are understanding of this change and willingly contribute to our work, but the main body of Ahousaht members, as well as many of our leaders, still do not know enough about our office. "What do you do? Why is it so important? How much does it cost us? Will we ever see the benefits from this program?" Many such questions are asked of the Ahousaht GIS Department.

We believe the answers to these questions lie in our mission. If we can bridge the knowledge gaps between generations, and help our people better manage our resources, we will help to make a difference for our children.

support 27 jobs. However, the scientific panel's prescription for world-class logging will by definition increase the number of jobs per thousand cubic metres because the panel calls for more sophisticated planning, and a more selective and less mechanized approach to logging. In addition, extra processing jobs can clearly be created through a concerted effort to add value to the raw resource before it leaves Clayoquot Sound. Finally, it is important to include into the calculation of harvestable area the potential for forests to regenerate. Assuming complete regeneration of areas that have already been cut, and applying the scientific panel's recommendations of re-harvesting only in environmentally and culturally appropriate areas, an additional 27,938.08 cubic metres will eventually come on stream for sustainable harvest. Thus, upon regeneration of already developed watersheds, the total sustainable yield in Clayoquot Sound will rise to 48,078.23 cubic metres per year, enough to *sustain* 65 jobs in perpetuity. It is the stated desire of government, industry, labour and local communities to log more responsibly, at a sustainable rate, and to promote value-added manufacturing. More than 20,000 cubic metres of wood a year is a sufficient base from which to start building a viable, selective, scientifically sanctioned, and sustainable logging and forest products industry in Clayoquot Sound, and to create forestry employment in perpetuity. The work in the woods can continue in Clayoquot Sound, and the war in the woods will finally be over when the pristine watersheds are given the protection they so richly deserve.

[28] Keith Moore, *Profiles of the Undeveloped Watersheds on Vancouver Island* (1991), 1-2, 8-21.

[29] Allan Chapman, Ministry of Forests, and Tony Cheong, Ministry of Environment, Lands and Parks, *Assessments of Developed Watersheds in Clayoquot Sound* (1995), iii-v.

1025

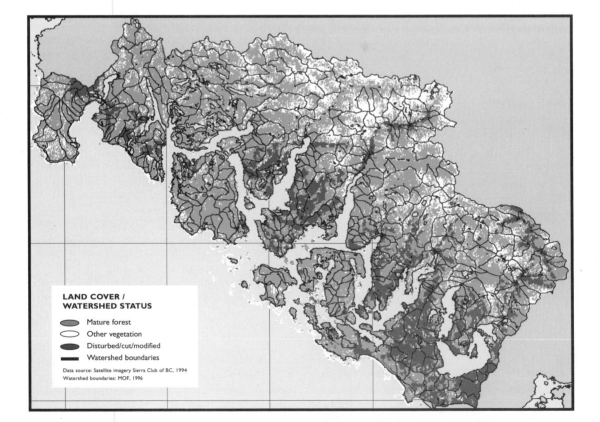

LAND COVER /
WATERSHED STATUS

- Mature forest
- Other vegetation
- Disturbed/cut/modified
- Watershed boundaries

Data source: Satellite imagery Sierra Club of BC, 1994
Watershed boundaries: MOF, 1996

Last Stands: The Pristine Watersheds of Clayoquot Sound

In the entire coastal temperate forest of British Columbia there are 354 primary watersheds (those that empty into the ocean) larger than 5,000 hectares. Of the 60 watersheds of this size on the west coast of Vancouver Island, only five are pristine— that is to say, showing virtually no evidence of human or industrial activity. Three of these five—the Sydney (5,885 ha), the Megin (24,300 ha) and the Moyeha (18,220 ha) are in the northern part of Clayoquot Sound.[28] Together they make up the largest contiguous area of undeveloped primary watersheds on Vancouver Island. Three large secondary Clayoquot Sound watersheds—the Ursus, upper Bulson and Clayoquot—are virtually pristine. The Moyeha watershed is protected as part of Strathcona Provincial Park, the Megin through the Clayoquot Sound land-use decision. The Ursus remains open to timber harvesting subject to protection of wildlife needs. The upper Sydney and Clayoquot, and the entire upper Bulson, remain open to development with no special requirements under the land-use decision to accommodate wildlife, recreation or scenic values.

The value of maintaining the integrity of these watersheds is far less easy to quantify than the economic worth of their timber. One cannot measure their cultural or spiritual significance to First Nations people, or the worth of undisturbed biodiversity in the natural ecosystem that an entire watershed represents. As the work of the Clayoquot Biosphere Project demonstrates, each watershed has entirely separate biological characteristics, and existing scientific understanding of the biological communities in intact watersheds is far too sparse to begin to draw conclusions about the needs of the species they contain.

The value of intact watersheds to the tourism industry cannot be determined solely on the basis of existing tourism activities. Currently, the economic potential of forests to tourism is measured primarily according to their scenic value. But people drawn to wilderness value the experience of being in a forest as much as looking at it from a distance. This is especially true in the Pacific Northwest, the fastest-growing region in North America. As long as the assumption persists that forests held in tree farm licences are unavailable for purposes other than timber production, any vision of the true long-term economic potential of wilderness will remain blocked. It is important to keep in mind that, as publicly owned land, tree farm licences may at some time return to public use. Yet once pristine or near-pristine valleys are developed, their value as wilderness is diminished, if not destroyed.

One way of appreciating the value of the intact watersheds of Clayoquot Sound is to consider the consequences of development elsewhere. A recent study of 12 developed watersheds in Clayoquot Sound found that the majority had suffered a high level of stream channel and riparian disturbance from woody debris, bank erosion, loss of shading, and slash and gravel dams. Logging-induced landslides have dumped sediments that take years to pass through stream systems.[29] The staggering decline in runs of spawning salmon in Clayoquot Sound streams must be attributed at least in part to industrial forestry's contribution to the destruction of their habitat. It must be remembered that much of this damage occurred during years when the forest industry trumpeted its high standards. Now, as a result of the scientific panel recommendations, those standards will undoubtedly be far higher. But is it worth taking the risk when so little is left and so much remains to be learned about the true effects of human intervention in undisturbed ecosystems? 106¶

In 1992 it was estimated that each 100,000 cubic metres of Clayoquot Sound timber would create 45 person years of woods employment for residents of the Alberni-Clayoquot region, and 69 person years of timber processing jobs.[30] On this basis, it takes about 1,000 cubic metres, or approximately 30 logging-truck loads, to create slightly more than one direct job. This is a high price to pay for future human enjoyment and employment—let alone the inherent value of undisturbed forest—in the 107¶ last pristine watersheds.

Clayoquot Sound's intact watersheds are among the few remaining unlogged valleys on Vancouver Island and there is an urgent need to protect them. One consequence of doing so will be to restore timber production to its traditional significance in the lives of the people of Clayoquot Sound. That is, the anomalous over-exploitation of timber in the twentieth century will end, and Clayoquot Sound will return to its traditions as a marine-based society in which the resources of the forests are simply one of many elements in a complex and diverse economy. The role of science will change accordingly. The importance of ocean resources—too often overlooked in the past bias towards forestry—speaks to the need for a scientific panel to conduct a compre- 108¶ hensive study of marine ecosystems.

As for the last unlogged watersheds, they will continue to be laboratories for world-class research, such as that already being undertaken by the Clayoquot Biosphere Project. A century ago, all but a few large watersheds on Vancouver Island were untouched by industrial development. Those that remain are all the more precious because of their rarity. Once developed, watersheds cannot be restored to their natural state by generations to come who may value undisturbed ecosystems far more than we do today. The decision to destroy the pristine character of any Clayoquot Sound watershed can only be made once. The price of doing so may be simply unaffordable. Finally, protecting the pristine watersheds of Clayoquot Sound is a fundamental demand of environmentalists if they are to continue supporting efforts to create a UNESCO Man and the Biosphere Reserve. Failure to protect the pristine watersheds will invite a return to protests, blockades and a continued international campaign to embarrass government and industry in key markets for Canadian forest products.[31] So the pristine watersheds must be protected and—according to the analysis presented above—can be protected without compromising Clayoquot Sound's ability to provide forest sector employment. The key difference is that in the new economy of Clayoquot Sound, the forest sector will no longer be such a dominant and distorting factor and, for the first time in decades, it will be truly sustainable 109¶ and a source of economic stability for local communities.

[30]Holman, Gary. "Socio-Economic Assessment of Land Use Options for the Clayoquot Sound Area." (October 1992), 12.

[31]"Victoria pushes biosphere status of Clayoquot Sound," *Vancouver Sun,* December 20, 1996, A1.

Setting the Boundaries:
A Plan for World-Class Logging

BY DAVID CARRUTHERS

In making good on the provincial government's promise to design "world-class" logging standards in Clayoquot Sound, the scientific panel is credited with having turned logging on its head in British Columbia. The panel reversed the traditional focus on timber supply, and demanded instead that ecosystem sustainability be the key factor that drives any development plans in the Sound. In keeping with this shift in thinking, Ecotrust Canada has turned mapping on its head in Clayoquot Sound. Rather than mapping for operability of forest stands, we have produced maps that detail the constraints to logging that are required if the ecosystem sustainability called 110¶ for by the scientific panel is to be achieved.

A detailed explanation of the methodology and limitations of our analysis appears as Appendix A. The maps should be read in conjunction with Appendix A, but can also 111¶ be understood with reference to the summary that appears below.

Using primarily existing government data, our maps progress as follows:

Map 1   indicates where no harvesting should occur in order to keep the rate-of-cut in particular watersheds within sustainable limits;

Map 2   shows reserves to protect sensitive and highly valued hydroriparian ecosystems;

Map 3   outlines protection required for unstable slopes;

Map 4   indicates reserves to protect late successional forest with forest-interior conditions;

Map 5   outlines important cultural values;

Map 6   describes areas with high scenic and recreational values;

Map 7   denotes corridors for wildlife and to connect recreational use areas;

Map 8   outlines existing protected areas; and,

Map 9   is a composite map showing areas in Clayoquot Sound where logging should not occur and areas, based on the scientific panel's recommendations, where sustainable forestry could potentially take place.

Map 10 combines all the above limits to logging and adds in one additional constraint, which is that there be no development of pristine or unlogged watersheds.

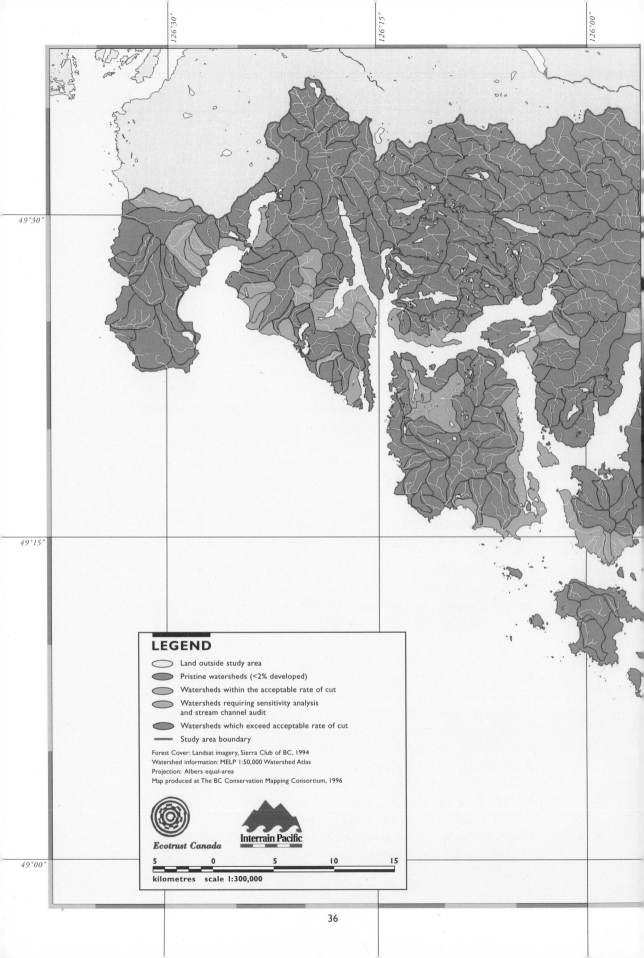

49°30"

49°15"

49°00"

LEGEND

- Land outside study area
- Pristine watersheds (<2% developed)
- Watersheds within the acceptable rate of cut
- Watersheds requiring sensitivity analysis and stream channel audit
- Watersheds which exceed acceptable rate of cut
- Study area boundary

Forest Cover: Landsat imagery, Sierra Club of BC, 1994
Watershed information: MELP 1:50,000 Watershed Atlas
Projection: Albers equal-area
Map produced at The BC Conservation Mapping Consortium, 1996

Ecotrust Canada

Interrain Pacific

5   0   5   10   15

kilometres   scale 1:300,000

Map I: Rate-of-Cut Classification for Watersheds in Clayoquot Sound

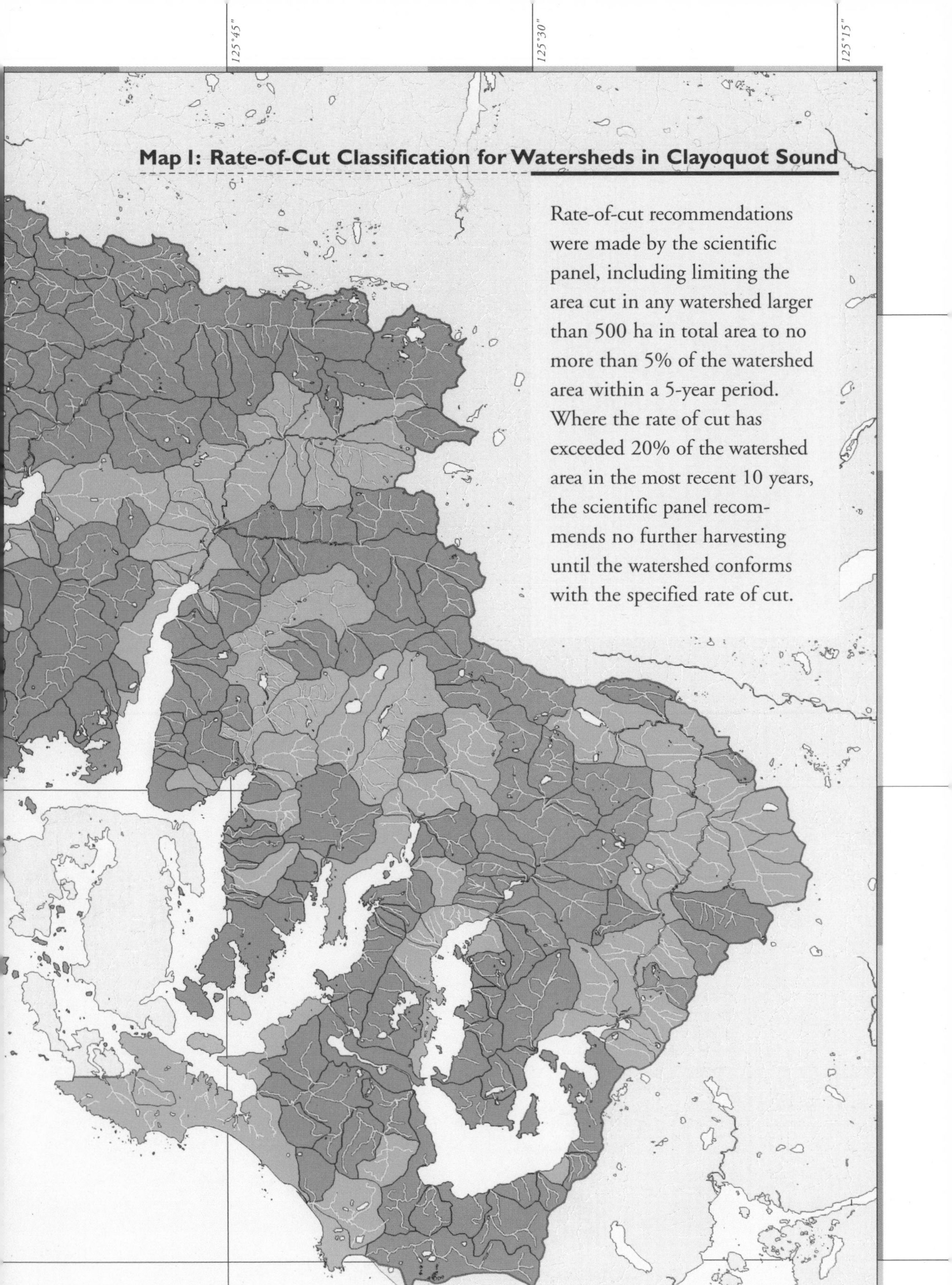

Rate-of-cut recommendations were made by the scientific panel, including limiting the area cut in any watershed larger than 500 ha in total area to no more than 5% of the watershed area within a 5-year period. Where the rate of cut has exceeded 20% of the watershed area in the most recent 10 years, the scientific panel recommends no further harvesting until the watershed conforms with the specified rate of cut.

Coordinate labels along the map borders:

126°30" 126°15" 126°00"

49°30"

49°15"

49°00"

LEGEND

Study Area
Land outside study area
Floodplains (100 m buffer)
Lakes, buffered
Wetlands, buffered
Streams and stream, buffered
Shoreline, buffered
Study area boundary

Primary data source: TRIM 1:20,000 base maps
Base information: MELP 1:50,000 Watershed Atlas
Projection: Albers equal-area
Map produced at The BC Conservation Mapping Consortium, 1996

Ecotrust Canada

Interrain Pacific

5   0   5   10   15

kilometres   scale 1:300,000

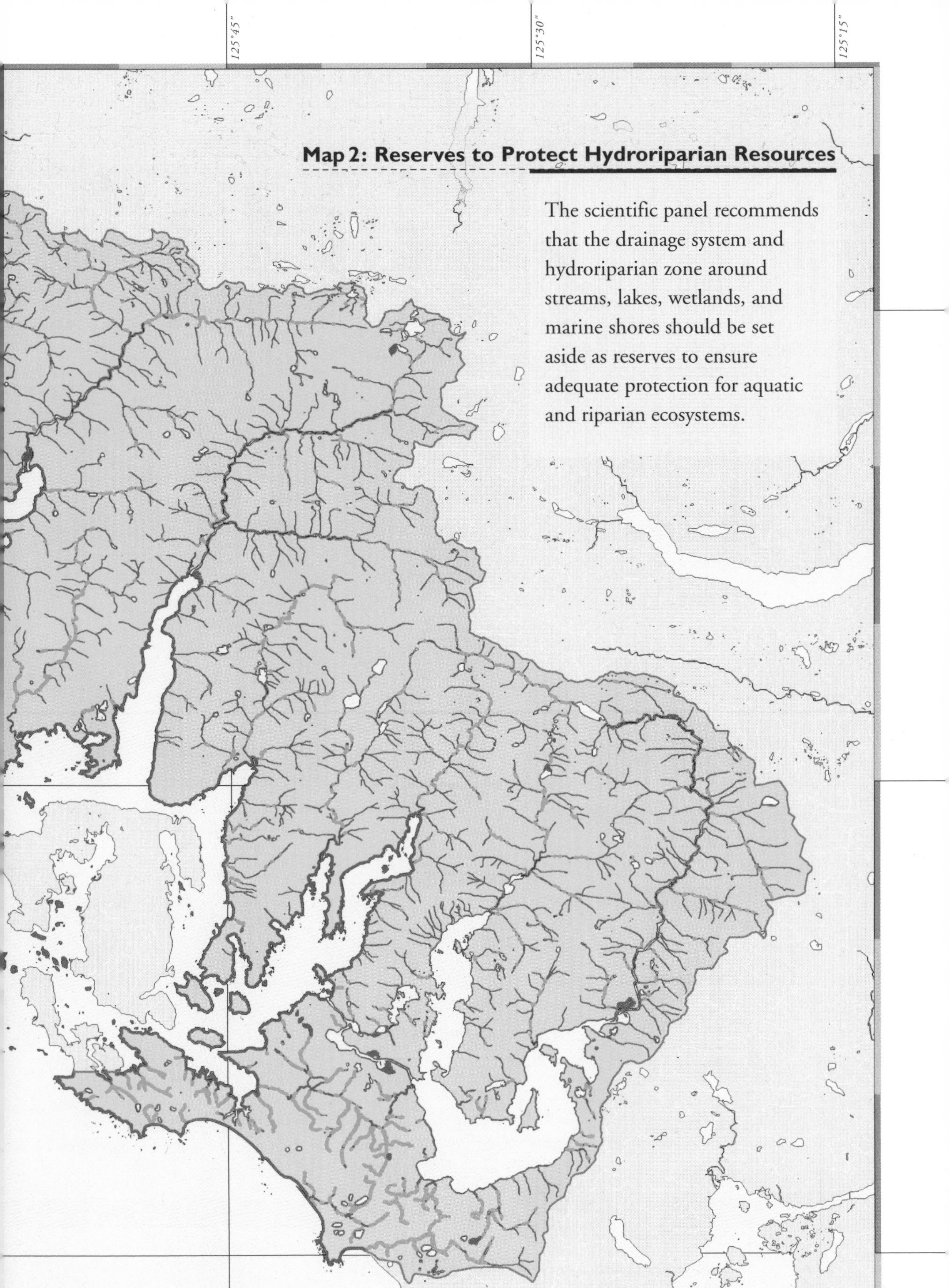

Map 2: Reserves to Protect Hydroriparian Resources

The scientific panel recommends that the drainage system and hydroriparian zone around streams, lakes, wetlands, and marine shores should be set aside as reserves to ensure adequate protection for aquatic and riparian ecosystems.

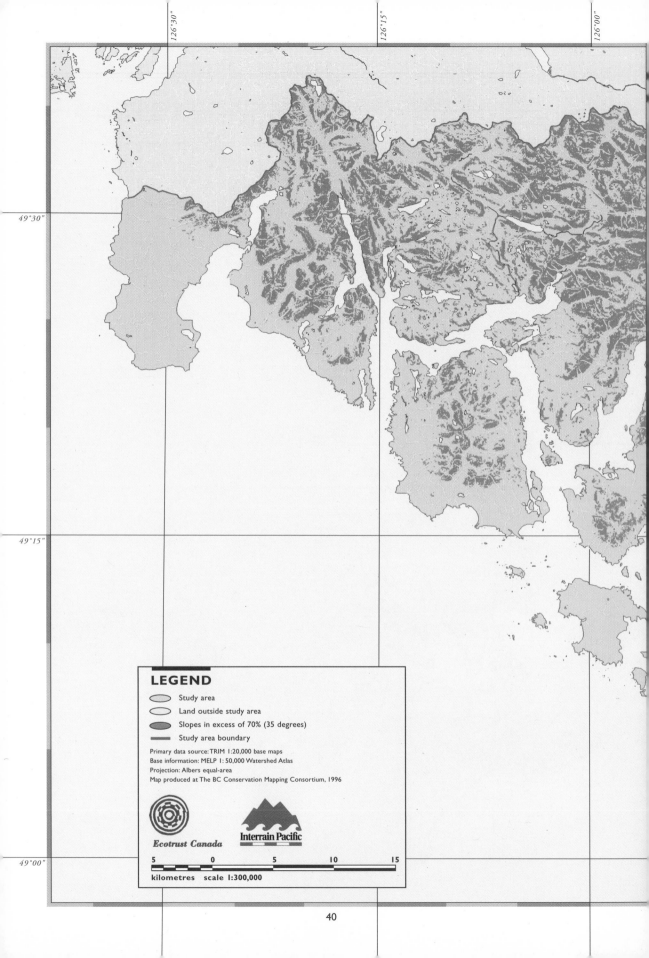

126°30"   126°15"   126°00"

49°30"

49°15"

49°00"

LEGEND

◯ Study area
◯ Land outside study area
◯ Slopes in excess of 70% (35 degrees)
─── Study area boundary

Primary data source: TRIM 1:20,000 base maps
Base information: MELP 1:50,000 Watershed Atlas
Projection: Albers equal-area
Map produced at The BC Conservation Mapping Consortium, 1996

Ecotrust Canada   Interrain Pacific

5   0   5   10   15

kilometres   scale 1:300,000

Map 3: Reserves to Protect Sensitive Soils and Unstable Terrain

The scientific panel stated that only stable terrain and resilient soils should be available for forest harvesting operations. Slopes in excess of 70% are generally regarded as areas prone to erosion and unsuitable for forest harvesting activities.

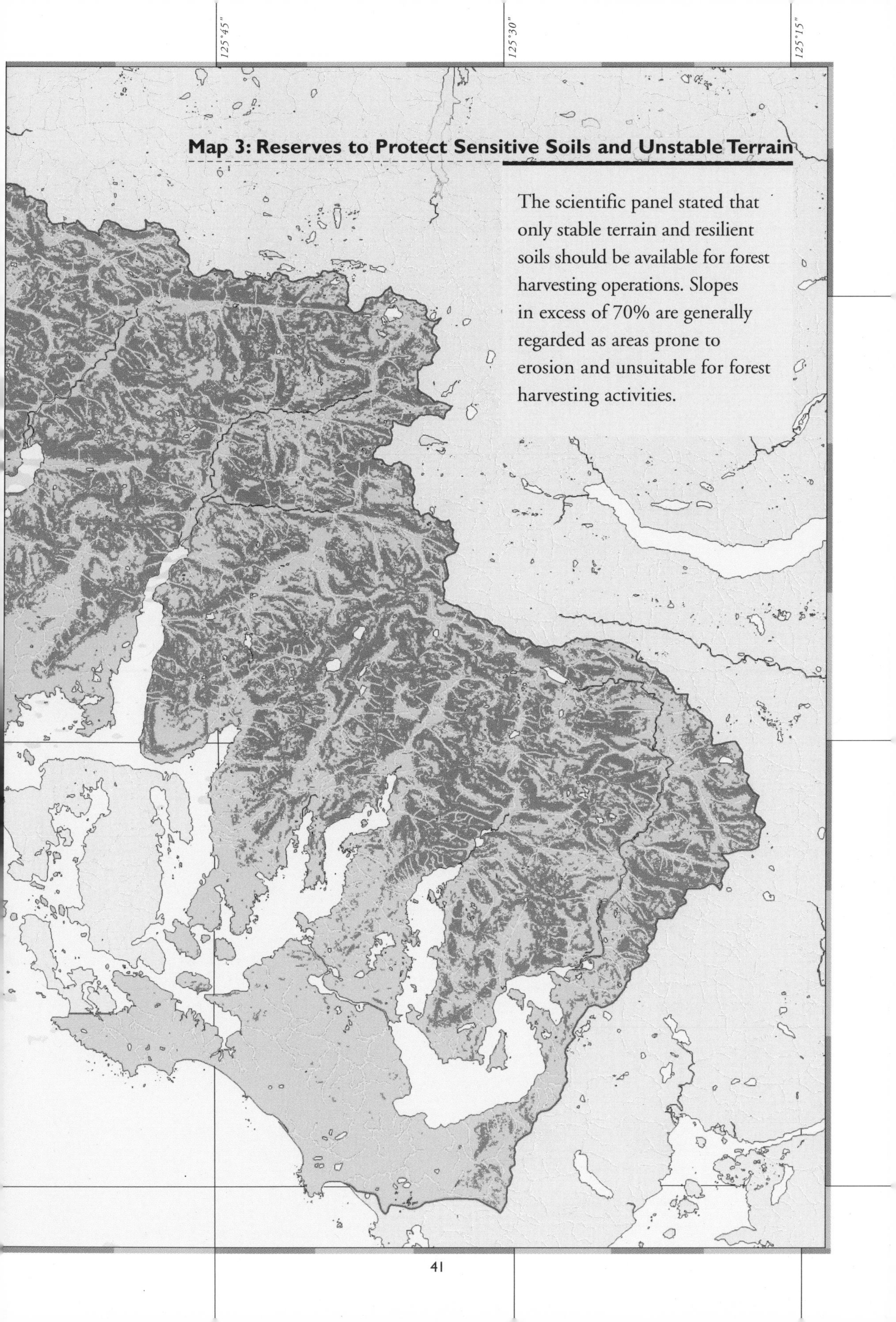

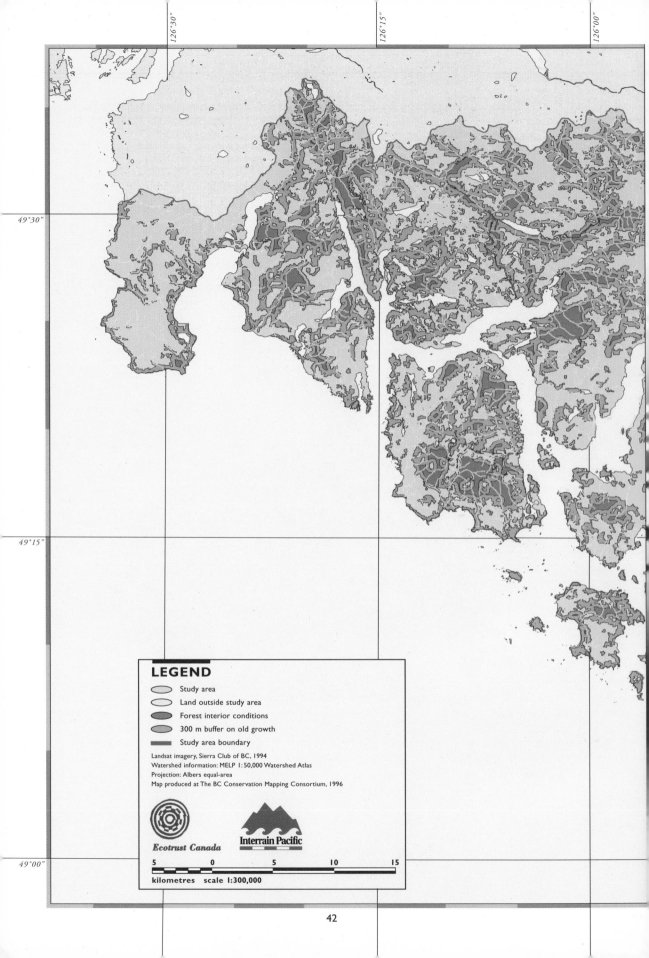

126°30" 126°15" 126°00"

49°30"

49°15"

49°00"

LEGEND

Study area
Land outside study area
Forest interior conditions
300 m buffer on old growth
Study area boundary

Landsat imagery, Sierra Club of BC, 1994
Watershed information: MELP 1:50,000 Watershed Atlas
Projection: Albers equal-area
Map produced at The BC Conservation Mapping Consortium, 1996

Ecotrust Canada   **Interrain Pacific**

5   0   5   10   15

kilometres   scale 1:300,000

Map 4: Reserves to Protect Forest-Interior Conditions

The scientific panel recommended that at least 40% of each watershed should be retained as class 8 and 9 forests (forests older than 141 years). Of this old growth, 20% should be retained as forest-interior conditions. Assuming tree heights of 50 m, the panel suggested using a 300 m buffer to delineate forest-interior conditions.

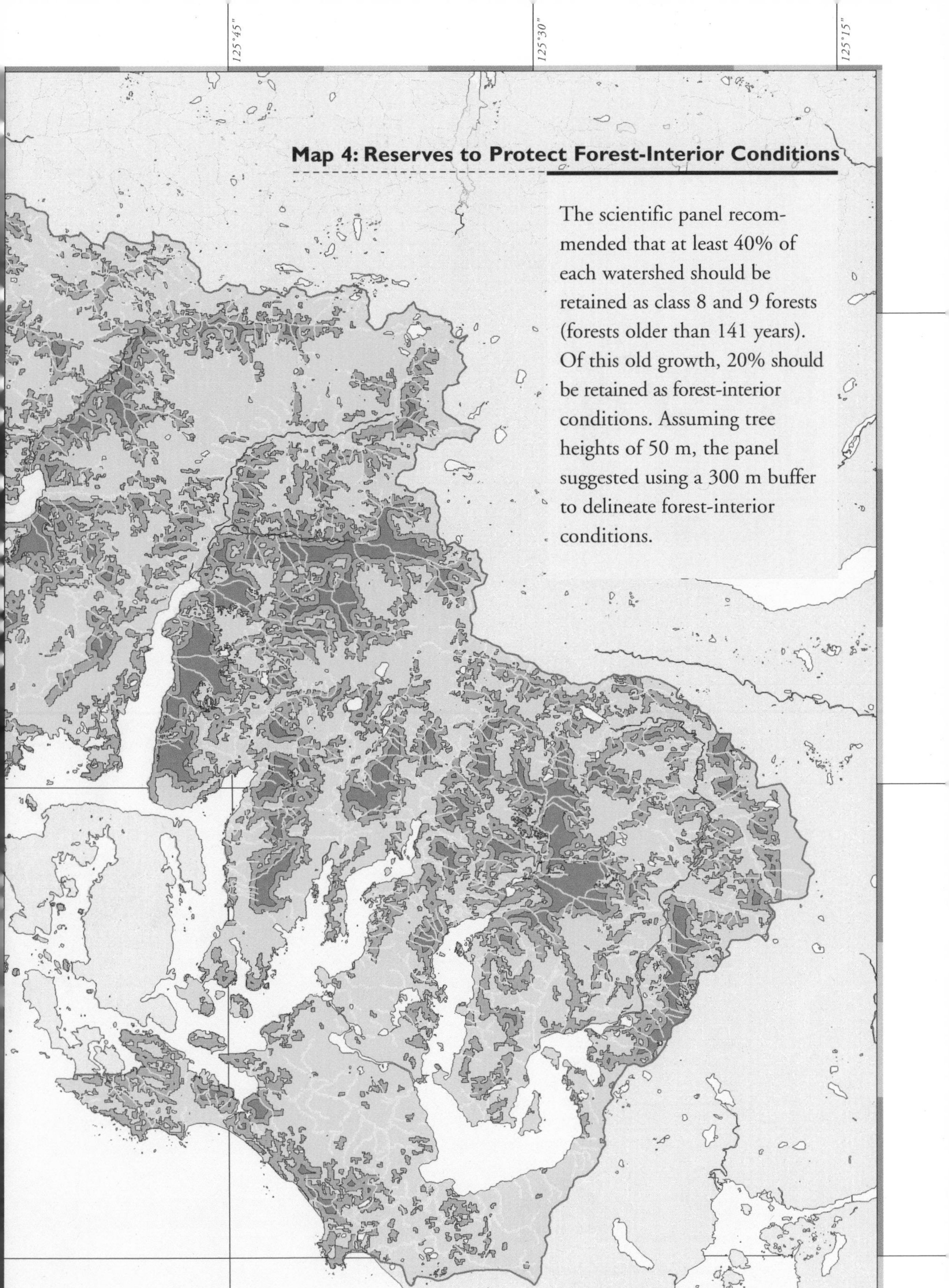

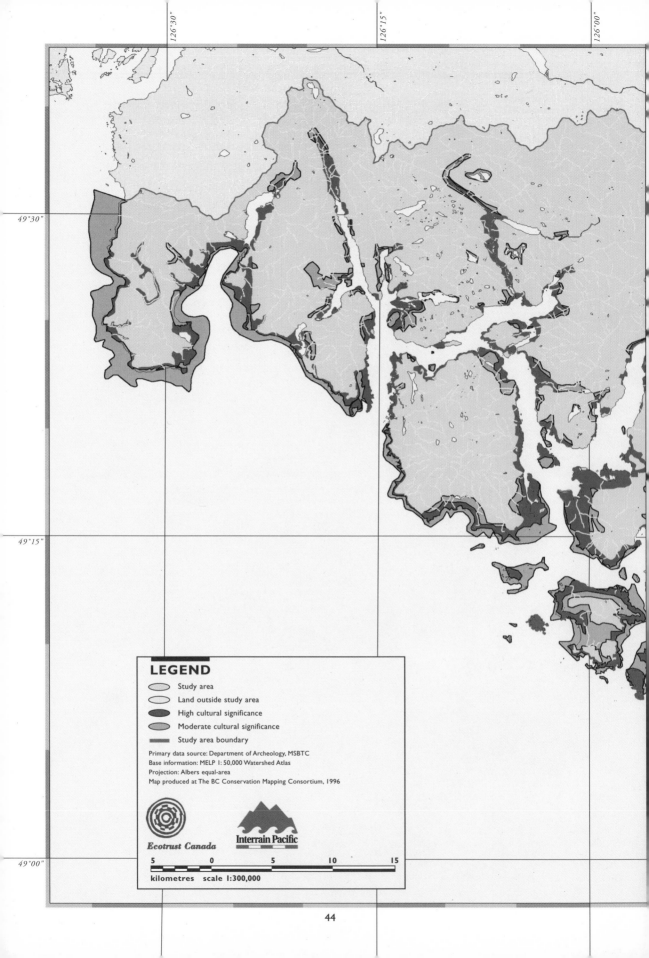

126°30"   126°15"   126°00"

49°30"

49°15"

49°00"

LEGEND

- Study area
- Land outside study area
- High cultural significance
- Moderate cultural significance
- Study area boundary

Primary data source: Department of Archeology, MSBTC
Base information: MELP 1: 50,000 Watershed Atlas
Projection: Albers equal-area
Map produced at The BC Conservation Mapping Consortium, 1996

Ecotrust Canada   **Interrain Pacific**

5   0   5   10   15

kilometres   scale 1:300,000

Map 5: Reserves to Protect Cultural Values

The scientific panel discussed a variety of culturally important areas which should be set aside as reserves, including sacred areas, historic areas and current use areas. These areas must be determined by the Nuu-chah-nulth nations and protected in ways consistent with traditional knowledge.

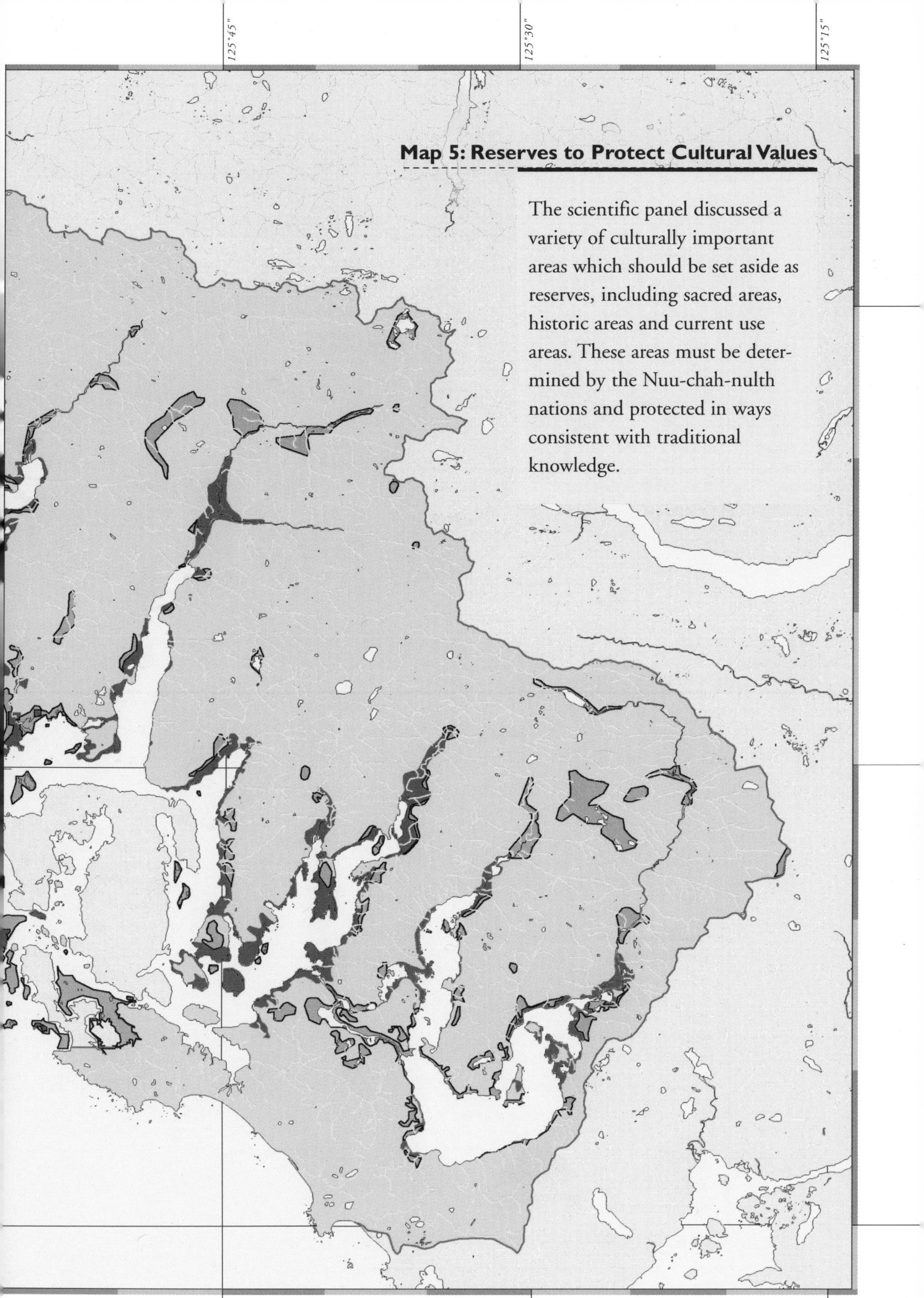

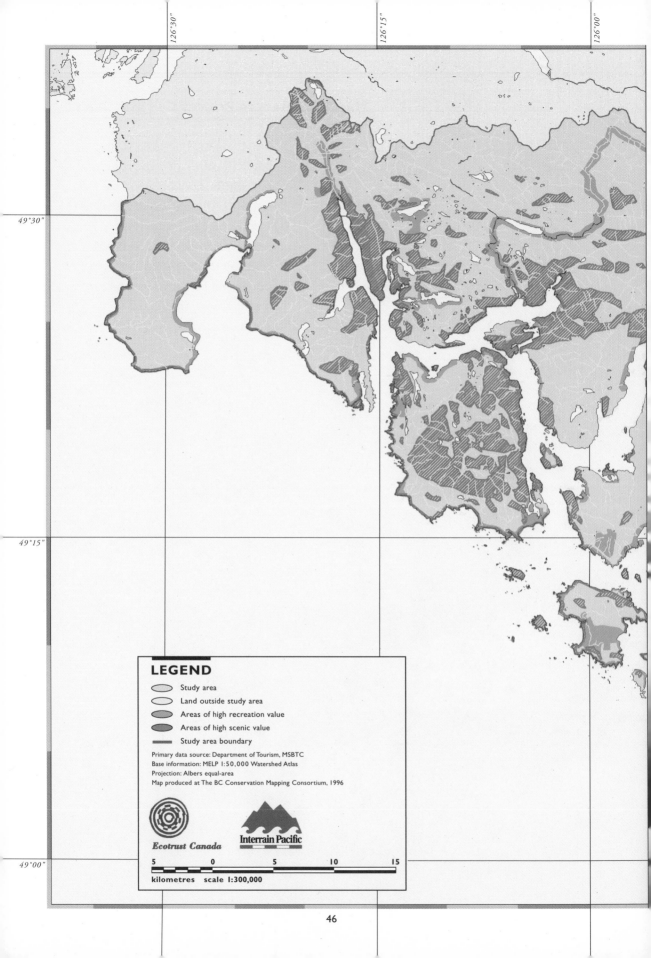

49°30"

49°15"

49°00"

LEGEND

Study area

Land outside study area

Areas of high recreation value

Areas of high scenic value

Study area boundary

Primary data source: Department of Tourism, MSBTC
Base information: MELP 1:50,000 Watershed Atlas
Projection: Albers equal-area
Map produced at The BC Conservation Mapping Consortium, 1996

Ecotrust Canada

Interrain Pacific

5   0   5   10   15

kilometres   scale 1:300,000

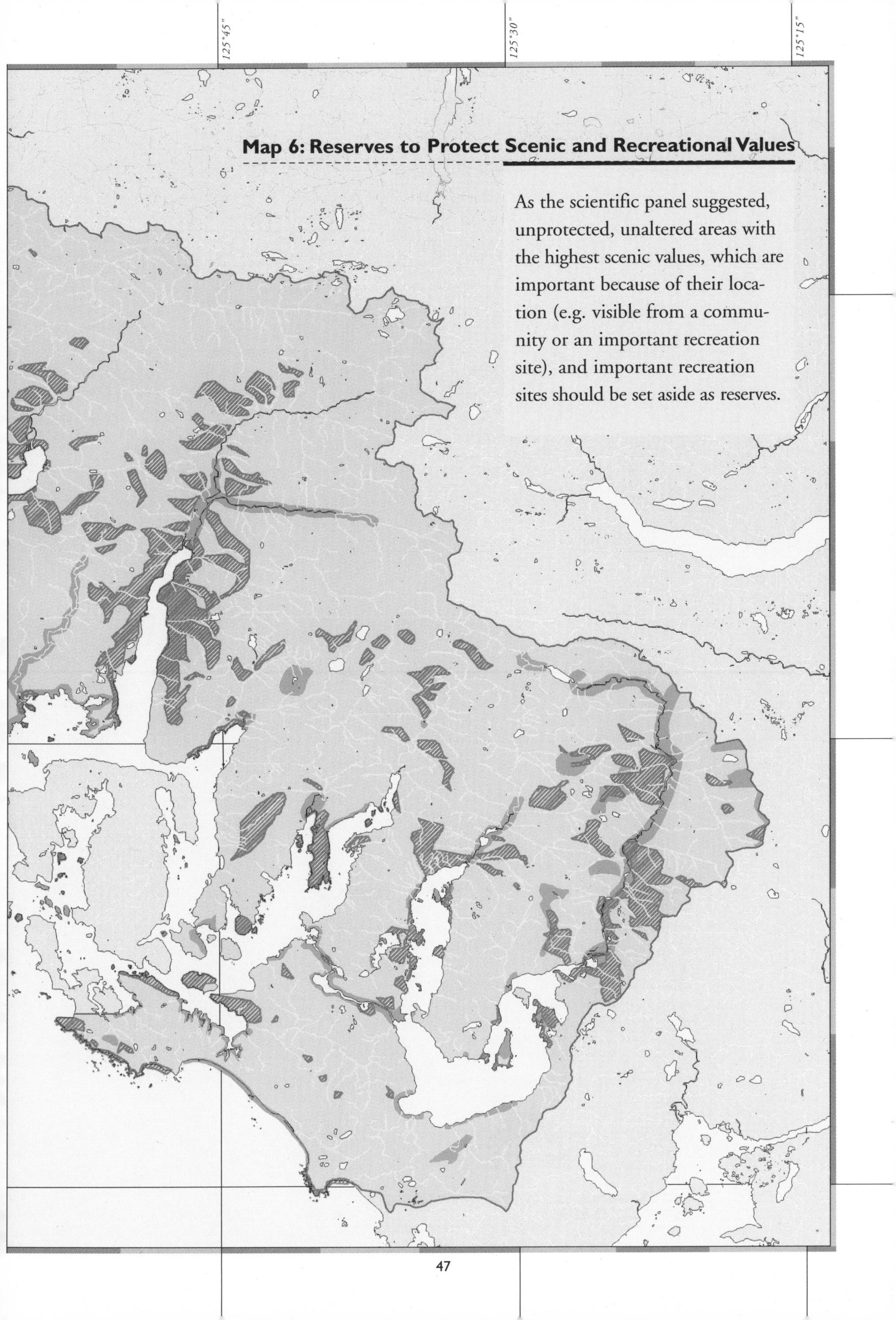

Map 6: Reserves to Protect Scenic and Recreational Values

As the scientific panel suggested, unprotected, unaltered areas with the highest scenic values, which are important because of their location (e.g. visible from a community or an important recreation site), and important recreation sites should be set aside as reserves.

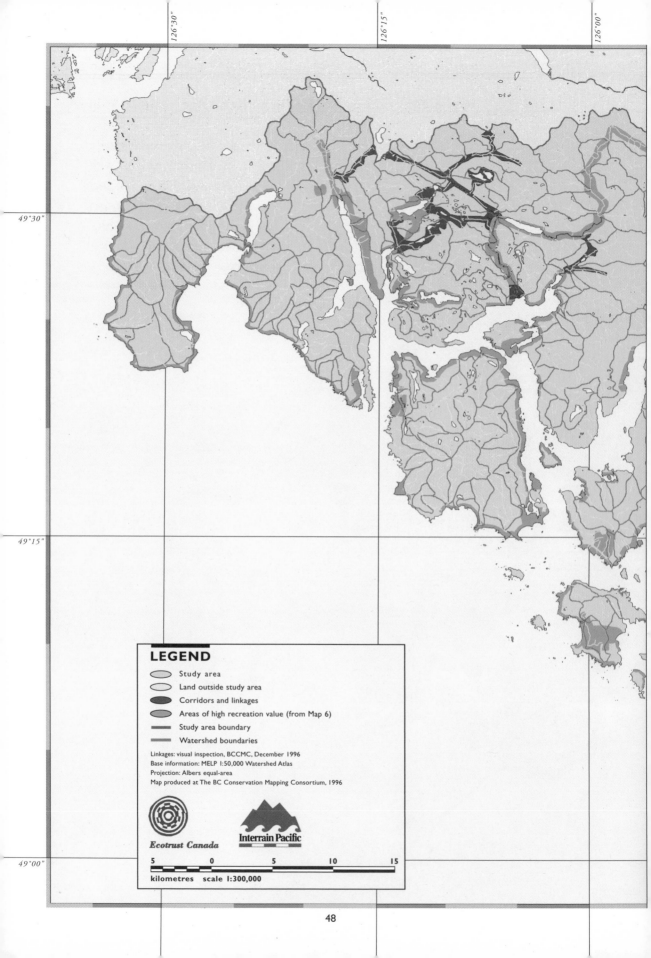

LEGEND

○ Study area
○ Land outside study area
● Corridors and linkages
● Areas of high recreation value (from Map 6)
— Study area boundary
— Watershed boundaries

Linkages: visual inspection, BCCMC, December 1996
Base information: MELP 1:50,000 Watershed Atlas
Projection: Albers equal-area
Map produced at The BC Conservation Mapping Consortium, 1996

Ecotrust Canada   **Interrain Pacific**

5   0   5   10   15

kilometres   scale 1:300,000

48

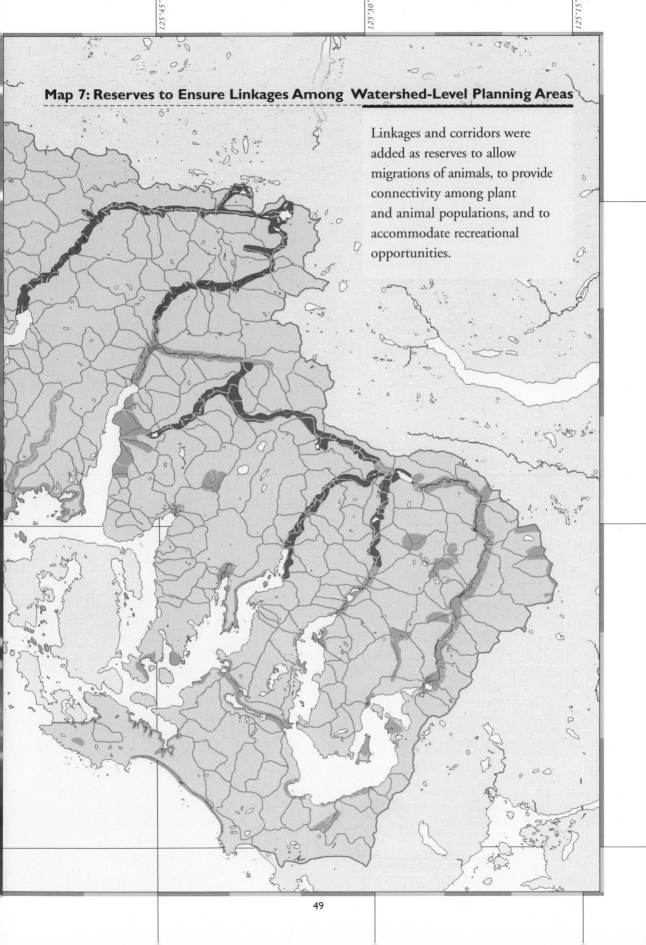

Map 7: Reserves to Ensure Linkages Among Watershed-Level Planning Areas

Linkages and corridors were added as reserves to allow migrations of animals, to provide connectivity among plant and animal populations, and to accommodate recreational opportunities.

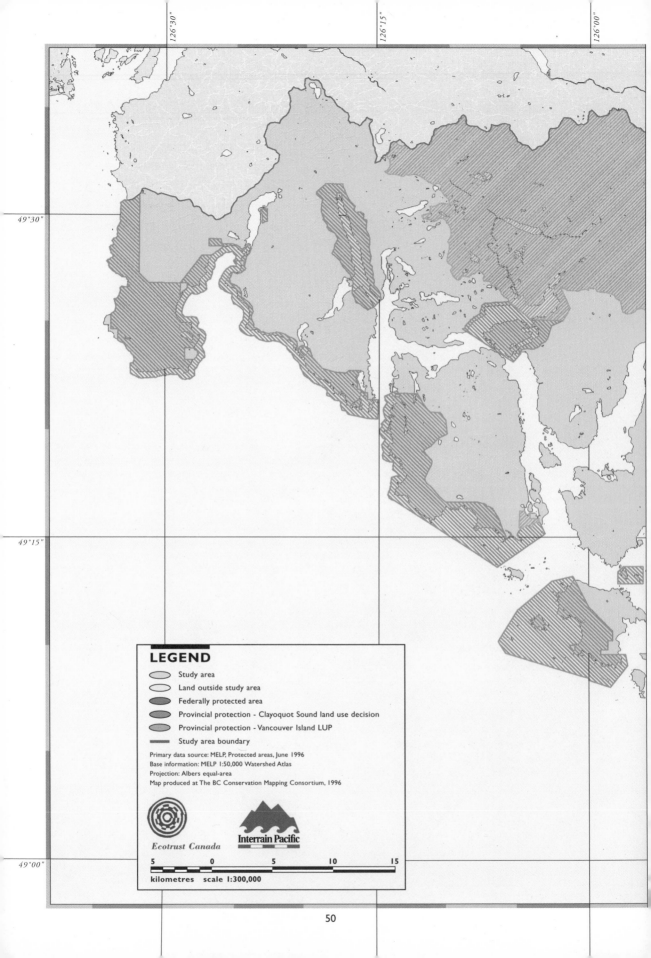

126°30" 126°15" 126°00"

49°30"

49°15"

49°00"

LEGEND

Study area
Land outside study area
Federally protected area
Provincial protection - Clayoquot Sound land use decision
Provincial protection - Vancouver Island LUP
Study area boundary

Primary data source: MELP, Protected areas, June 1996
Base information: MELP 1:50,000 Watershed Atlas
Projection: Albers equal-area
Map produced at The BC Conservation Mapping Consortium, 1996

Ecotrust Canada

Interrain Pacific

5   0   5   10   15

kilometres   scale 1:300,000

Map 8: Existing Protected Areas

In total, approximately one third of the land in Clayoquot Sound is presently set aside in protected areas. Of this, 48,500 ha was protected as a result of the 1993 Clayoquot Sound land use decision.

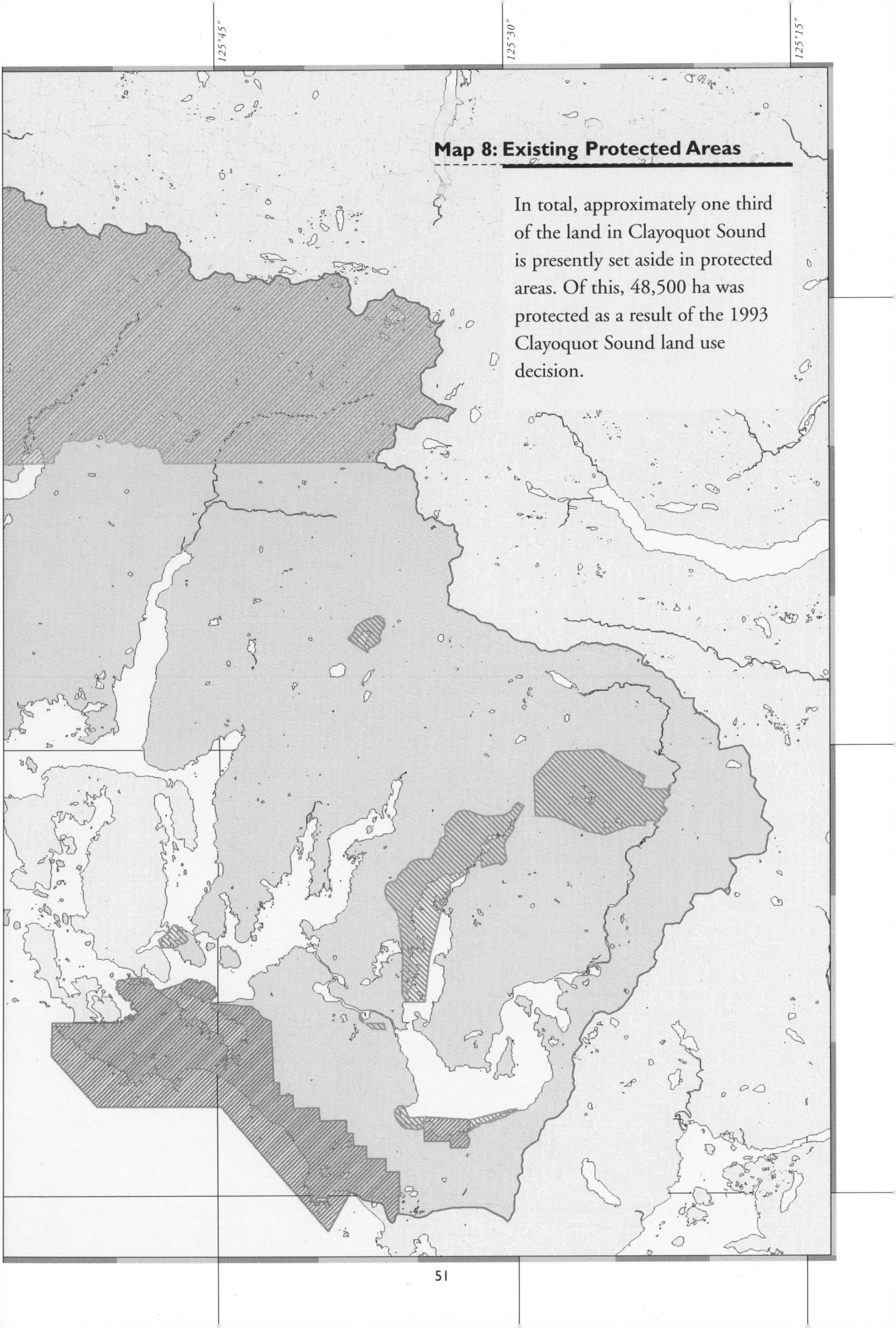

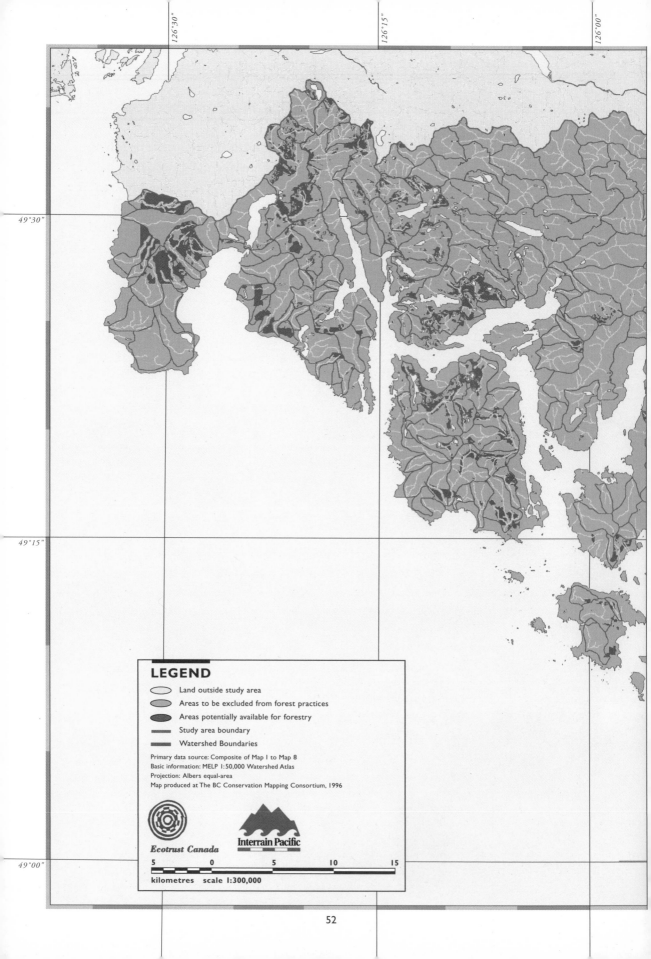

LEGEND

◯ Land outside study area

◯ Areas to be excluded from forest practices

◯ Areas potentially available for forestry

━━ Study area boundary

━━ Watershed Boundaries

Primary data source: Composite of Map 1 to Map 8
Basic information: MELP 1:50,000 Watershed Atlas
Projection: Albers equal-area
Map produced at The BC Conservation Mapping Consortium, 1996

Ecotrust Canada   **Interrain Pacific**

5   0   5   10   15

kilometres   scale 1:300,000

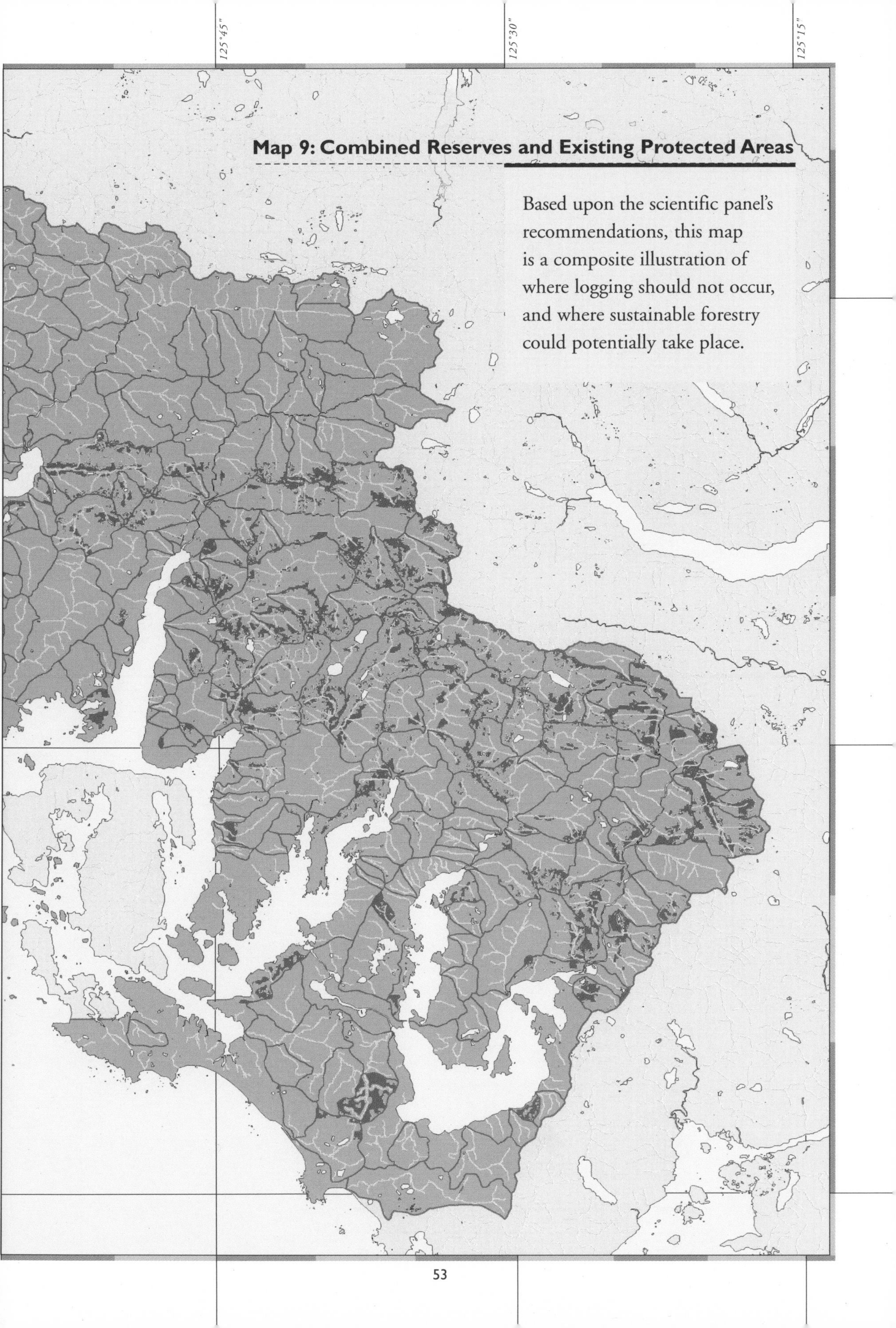

Map 9: Combined Reserves and Existing Protected Areas

Based upon the scientific panel's recommendations, this map is a composite illustration of where logging should not occur, and where sustainable forestry could potentially take place.

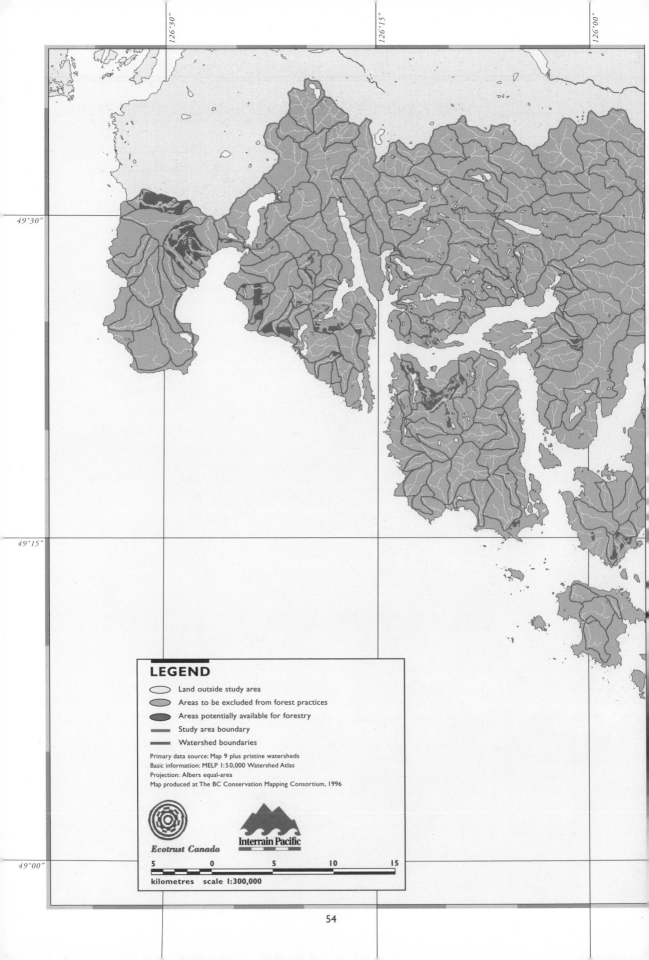

LEGEND

- ⬭ Land outside study area
- ⬭ Areas to be excluded from forest practices
- ⬭ Areas potentially available for forestry
- ▬ Study area boundary
- ▬ Watershed boundaries

Primary data source: Map 9 plus pristine watersheds
Basic information: MELP 1:50,000 Watershed Atlas
Projection: Albers equal-area
Map produced at The BC Conservation Mapping Consortium, 1996

Ecotrust Canada   **Interrain Pacific**

5   0   5   10   15

kilometres   scale 1:300,000

126°30"   126°15"   126°00"

49°30"

49°15"

49°00"

54

Map 10: Combined Reserves, Existing Protected Areas and Pristine Watersheds

There exists a widespread belief that the remaining untouched watersheds in Clayoquot Sound should be protected from development. This map illustrates the previous composite constraints map with the additional constraint that there be no development in pristine watersheds.

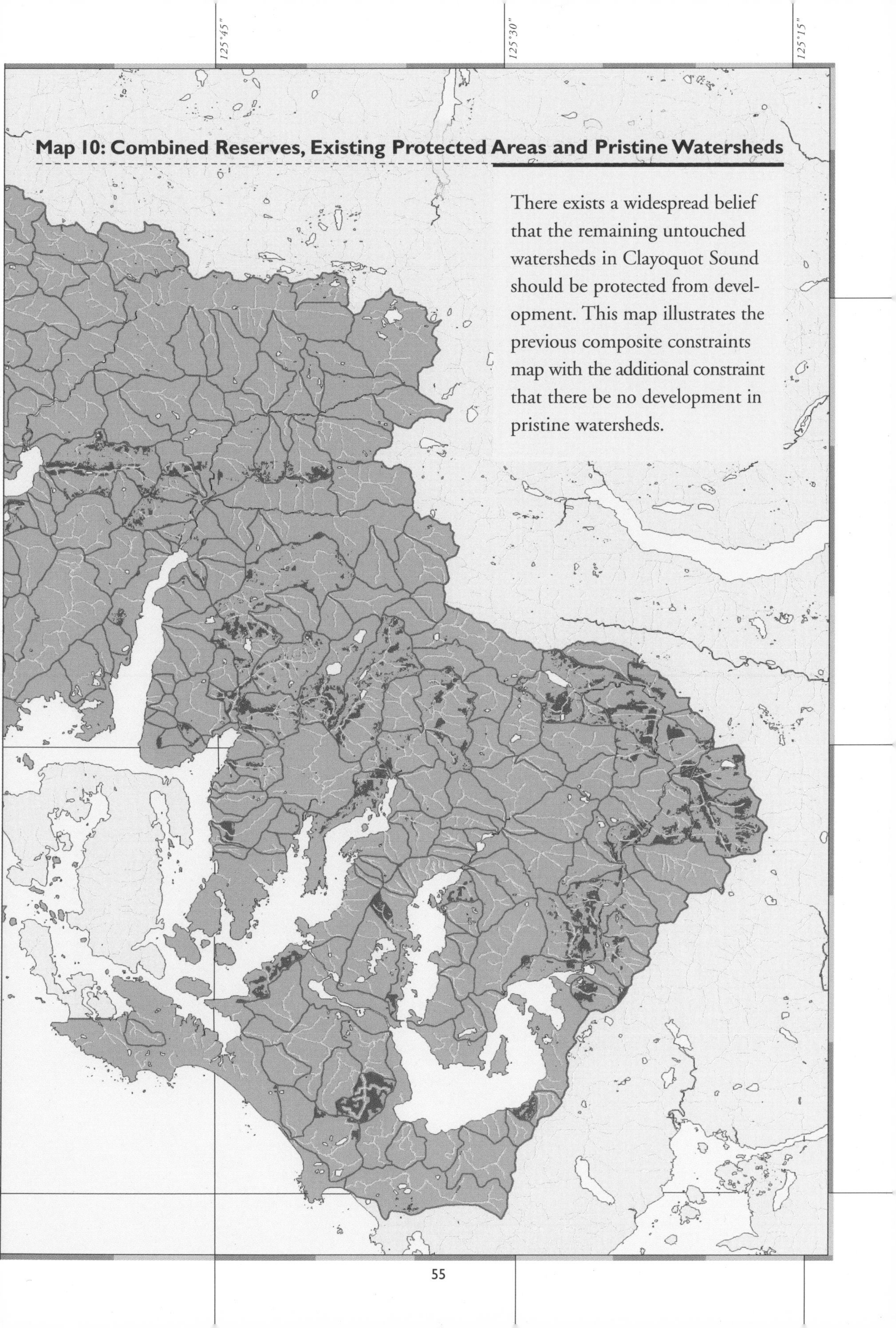

Strength in Diversity:
Building the New Economy

BY DAVID GREER AND KATRINA KUCEY

The pattern of economic activities in Clayoquot Sound has undergone significant shifts during the last two decades. Declines in the commercial fishing and forest industries have been accompanied by an expansion of the tourist industry—once primarily focused on Pacific Rim National Park and bolstered in recent years by an increasing interest among visitors in trips to the heart of Clayoquot Sound. Salmon-farming, a recent addition to the economy, now provides more than 200 full-time jobs but is surrounded by controversy about its potential impacts on marine ecosystems. Shellfish farming is another developing industry with enormous potential. Small businesses in value-added forestry produce a variety of products, and markets
112¶ show promise for further expansion.

For all this activity and potential for diversity, the economy of Clayoquot Sound is going nowhere fast. Land and fresh water—for tourism facilities, industrial sites, seafood processing, and housing—are in short supply. Value-added wood operations often have great ambitions but little hope of getting their hands on the waste wood they need to run a business. Forest land remains locked in tree farm licences that are largely unavailable for uses other than timber production. Shellfish farmers are hampered by the absence of local processing facilities. Nuu-chah-nulth initiatives to diversify the economies of First Nation communities are frustrated by ongoing uncertainty over treaty negotiations and by unemployment rates that often exceed 70 per cent. And efforts to restore health to the fishing industry by increasing local control in fisheries management remain stymied amid finger-pointing between higher levels
113¶ of government and conflicting theories about how to bring the salmon back.

The economy of Clayoquot Sound has taken a beating in recent years. There is no shortage of ideas and initiative in local communities for a diversified, ocean-based economy that can prosper without depleting resources or degrading the environment. In a variety of innovative ventures, and despite continuing obstacles, the residents of Clayoquot Sound are attempting to build the foundation for a conservation-based
114¶ economy. They need and deserve all the support they can get.

A TERRIBLE TOLL

Collapses in fishing and sea-hunting industries—
West Coast of Vancouver Island

1820s	Sea otters
1900s	Fur-seals
1920s	Humpback whales
1940s	Pilchards
1950s	Halibut
1960s	Herring
1960s	Chinook, coho, chum, sockeye
1980s	Abalone

Fisheries—Turning the Tide

Twenty years ago life in Tofino and Ucluelet revolved around the docks, where local fishermen set out each morning in day-boats, confident of returning hours later with a good haul of salmon, just as their fathers and grandfathers might have done before them. Those days are gone. The life of troll fishers today is one of the most stressful on the west coast. Many have sold their boats; some have converted them for other uses, such as guiding whale-watching tours. "It used to be that if a fisherman had a bad year, he'd shrug it off, knowing the next year might be good and make up for it," says a former troller. "Now nobody can count on a good year any more, and there's a depressed attitude right through the industry." 115¶

All six species of salmon stocks on the west coast— coho, chinook, sockeye, pink, chum and steelhead—have been in decline for several decades. Efforts to understand the reasons why have been frustrated by a lack of knowledge of the habits and habitat needs of fish whose ocean travels extend hundreds and in some cases thousands of miles from their spawning streams and that include several thousand genetically distinct stocks, most of 116¶ them associated with an individual river.

Roughly three-quarters of all salmon returning to spawn in British Columbia streams are caught by the commercial, sports and aboriginal fisheries. Bigger boats and more efficient equipment are only two of several factors implicated in the depletion of salmon stocks. Spawning habitat in hundreds of streams has been damaged or destroyed by urbanization and poor logging practices. Heavy catches in US waters, especially by Alaskan fleets, have been blamed for threatening BC salmon runs, just as the BC catch has been blamed for declines in Oregon and Washington. Ocean warming, associated with the periodic shift in sea surface temperatures known as El Niño, is another possible cause. The bottom line is that salmon are disappearing from many streams, and for reasons numerous enough to make the assignment of blame a complex matter. The challenge now is not to lay blame for what has happened, but to assign responsibility for restoring salmon stocks and for managing them judiciously. 117¶

The salmon fishery is merely the latest example of many that have sustained the Clayoquot Sound economy in the past, only to falter as stocks disappeared. After the first whaling station opened in Barkley Sound in 1905, it took only 15 years to virtually eliminate the humpback—dispatched by mechanical harpoons that achieved in moments what the Nuu-chah-nulth had once taken several days to do with ceremony, skill, and raw courage. The 1940s saw the total disappearance of pilchards—a fishery

32 Terry Glavin, *Dead Reckoning: Confronting the Crisis in Pacific Fisheries* (Vancouver: Douglas & McIntyre, 1996), 53.

33 Ibid., 64.

34 Entech Environmental Consultants, "Sustainable Development of the Aquaculture and Fisheries Sectors in Clayoquot Sound, BC " (prepared for Clayoquot Sound Sustainable Development Strategy Steering Committee, 31 March 1991), 7, 10.

that only a decade earlier had been the third largest in the province after salmon and herring. By the 1950s the halibut banks off the west coast of the island had been practically fished out, and in the 1960s herring were virtually eliminated after seine nets proved too effective a tool. The disappearance of the herring, a primary food in the salmon diet, was linked in turn to the collapse of chinook stocks. The herring later recovered; the chinook did not. Still later, even scuba diving took its toll, and the valuable abalone fishery was closed in 1990. Geoducks—large clams that bring handsome prices on the Japanese market—may well be next.

The depletion of economically valuable sea life on the west coast has often followed intensive fishing by outside interests with the ability to make large capital investments in new technologies. Today's deep-sea trawl fishery is a case in point. Almost 60 per cent of all the fish caught on the west coast are taken by trawlers, and more than half their catch is delivered to the US for processing.[32] Few Clayoquot Sound fishers participate in the industry, for the massive capital investment required for the giant boats and equipment is prohibitive; instead, the industry is largely run by Vancouver-based corporations. Called by some the ocean equivalent of strip mining, trawling is both non-selective and highly effective at taking everything that falls in the path of nets—some of them large enough to hold a passenger jet—that are often dragged directly along the ocean floor.

A study in the early 1980s found that up to 40 per cent of the fish caught by the BC trawl fleet are unwanted species that are thrown overboard.[33] This "bycatch" includes large numbers of salmon that cannot legally be kept by trawlers. Thus, the trawl fishery has become yet another factor contributing to the decline of salmon stocks. The industry's biggest catch is hake, a relative of the Pacific cod. Two hake-processing plants provide employment for about 300 workers in Ucluelet, but their future is uncertain. Increasingly, catch from the trawlers is being diverted for processing to US plants, where labour costs are lower than in Canada.

The trawl fishery illustrates both the extreme harvesting efficiency of some components of the fishing industry and the degree to which small coastal communities have gradually been marginalized in the Pacific fishery by the trend toward corporate concentration. Half the BC salmon catch is allocated to seine boats that are so efficient some fill their yearly quota in two weeks, moving among different areas of the coast. A significant number of the seiners are owned by large, vertically integrated firms with interests in the packing, processing and retail businesses as well.

For the most part, the economic value of fisheries in the Clayoquot Sound area is directed elsewhere. In 1990 the total landed value of all fish caught in Area 24 (Clayoquot Sound) was $14,615,467. By comparison, the estimated landed value to local communities from Area 24 and all other fishing areas on the coast was less than one-third of that amount.[34]

Many Clayoquot Sound fishers express frustration at the depletion of ocean resources by well-financed outside interests and by the Department of Fisheries and Oceans' apparent bias towards highly mechanized, heavily capitalized fisheries. One example of this type of misguided management, say the critics, is the brief openings that favour fast-travelling boats with sophisticated harvesting technologies. The roe herring fishery in Barkley Sound, open for only a matter of hours once a year, leads to a frantic scramble among seiners. Some local fishers argue that a longer-term fishery, limited to less efficient technologies such as gill-netting, would not only be effective in sustaining the fishery, but would have the added advantage of creating more employment and lending stability to local communities.

In 1996, the federal government announced a plan to halve the 4,200-boat BC fishing fleet by buying back vessel licences and restricting those that remained to specific areas of the coast rather than allowing coast-wide travel. The "Mifflin Plan" (named for federal fisheries minister Fred Mifflin) was roundly condemned in small coastal communities. The net effect of the plan, its critics said, would be to further concentrate industry control in the hands of operators of large vessels with sufficient capital to buy several licences, while squeezing out small-vessel owners. Their fears were proven justified in the months after the plan came into effect, as significantly larger numbers of licences were surrendered in rural communities, where fishers in a failing industry tended to be in more desperate need of cash and to have fewer economic alternatives than those in urban centres. The result has been a devastating impact on the economic base of coastal villages. A study commissioned by the BC government estimated that the Mifflin plan has cost 2,895 jobs in coastal communities.[35]

By perpetuating and indeed accelerating the trend towards corporate concentration, the Mifflin Plan has hastened the erosion of coastal community economies, and moreover seems doomed to fail in its professed intent to conserve salmon stocks. Licences have been reduced in number but are now concentrated among vessel-owners with the most sophisticated and efficient gear and the least incentive to conserve stocks. Rather than reducing the involvement of coastal communities in the fishery, it would make far more sense from both an economic and a conservation standpoint to start building a foundation for a greater community role in fisheries management.

One logical way of doing so would be to develop a system of community quotas, whereby fishing rights would be allocated to communities and distributed in turn to local fishers, in much the same way as timber-cutting rights are distributed in community forests. Through such a system, rural communities could apply their knowledge of local conservation issues and management needs in working to ensure both the sustainability of stocks and the sustainability of local economies. By providing the guarantee of long-term economic benefits to a community as a whole, community quotas would in turn foster a sense of community stewardship of resources. By contrast, the current system of fisheries management separates conservation responsibilities from fishing rights, pits individual fishers against one another, and perpetuates "the tragedy of the commons" in which the promotion of short-term individual profit over community cooperation and shared responsibility ensures the continued eradication of the natural capital that sustains communities.

In 1996 the BC and federal governments signed a Memorandum of Understanding that acknowledges changes are necessary in the management of the Pacific fishery and

123¶
124¶
125¶
126¶

[35] "Poor fish runs, fleet cutbacks cost 7,800 jobs, BC report says," *Vancouver Sun,* 9 October 1996, A1.

A NEW LINE ON FISH
By Dan Edwards

The Westcoast Sustainability Association (WCSA) is a community-based organization that promotes local stewardship of the fisheries. Working on many fronts, the WCSA aims to create economic and conservation opportunties that are pegged to local involvement in resource management and harvesting. Today it functions as a political organization and operates a storefront office in Ucluelet, which it shares with the Coastal Communities Network.

The WCSA advocates the local entitlement of coastal communities to west coast fisheries and their management. Since 1995 the constituency of the WCSA has expanded to include commercial fishers, residents, sportfishers, the Nuu-chah-nulth Tribal Council, academics, the Coastal Communities Network and more recently the Pacific Salmon Alliance. Each of these constituents has a different and deep-felt interest in coastal fisheries, and all have an important stake in how they are managed.

The WCSA has been a springboard for a number of positive local initiatives that have brought people together in the name of stewardship and community stability. The association does this in a number of ways, ranging from salmon enhancement at Thornton Creek and Kennedy Lake, to strong advocacy for fisheries co-management via the formation of a Regional Resources Management Board.

Ideally the management board will function as a sort of locally controlled Department of Fisheries and Oceans. The BC government is in discussion with the federal government on some transfer of authority for fisheries management to the province, and the WCSA wants to inject the concept of regional management into that discussion.

The idea is to provide a bridge between the centralized DFO management system on the one hand, and non-native commercial fishers, fishing communities, First Nations, and the provincial government on the other. If achieved, this would create the first unimposed, native/non-native community-based fisheries management system in British Columbia. Building blocks have been set in place over the past two years through discussion with Nuu-chah-nulth Tribal Council on developing a fisheries database

that would best serve the needs of the people living within the Nuu-chah-nulth region. On a broader regional level, the WCSA is working with the Pacific Salmon Alliance and Coastal Communities Network to promote this new community-based management system for coastal fisheries.

The scale of WCSA activities jumped in 1996 upon announcement of the federal Mifflin Plan, which aimed at reducing the Pacific salmon fleet through a buy-back of licenses, and the reorganizing of west coast fisheries around an area-based system. The WCSA believes the Mifflin Plan is a disaster for coastal communities, in that it will make fishing a rich man's game that is far too expensive for local operators and small-scale enterprises to even play, let alone win. The WCSA fears the Mifflin Plan will lead to further corporatization of the industry, and away from increased stewardship, local involvement and community economic stability that west coast fisherfolk are demanding. Already this fear is being borne out, as evidenced by the amalgamation of BC Packers and the Canadian Fish Co. in the summer of 1996.

As an antidote to concentration of the fisheries, the WCSA is working to rehabilitate wild salmon, and is researching community management of the trawl fishery. While the WCSA is breaking new ground on many levels, its deepest impact has been felt in its home community of Ucluelet, where residents have endured dramatic job losses in forestry and fishing since 1989. At the peak of residents' frustration over diminishing local control of livelihood opportunities, the WCSA was there as one of few means of building community unity and support for a positive future. Since 1992, the mandate has broadened to support a number of initiatives aiming at community economic and ecosystem stability, including a Holistic Resource Management community visioning process involving Ucluelet residents in 1996.

The WCSA sees an important role for itself continuing to build bridges between the aboriginal and non-aboriginal communities in the Nuu-chah-nulth territory through the promotion of governance models—such as a Regional Fisheries Management Board—that will represent all community interests. The need for these processes will become more urgent as the treaty process works toward substantive issues of resource ownership and control.

The communities of Clayoquot Sound have seen their fisheries resources managed largely for the benefit of outside interests, to their own detriment.

that there should be an enhanced role for the province. Under the memorandum, governments are reviewing the roles and responsibilities for fisheries management. To complement these negotiations, the province is developing a fisheries renewal strategy with three primary goals: sustaining and restoring fish habitat and stocks; increasing and diversifying employment in the fishing industry; and sustaining the well-being of coastal communities by ensuring a diversity of opportunities, promoting community-based shared decision-making, and encouraging local 127¶ investment and stewardship.

The strategy will represent a positive step towards resolving BC's fisheries crisis if it achieves its objectives of developing a comprehensive shared vision that has broad public support, ensuring greater coordination in federal and provincial fisheries management, and creating new institutions and consultative mechanisms that more actively involve local communities and stakeholders in decision-making. In the past, the confusing division of fisheries responsibilities between federal and provincial governments, and the absence of a strong role for coastal communities in the development of fisheries policy, have discouraged the efficient and comprehensive approach that is needed to restore the coastal fishery to health. Coordination of government efforts, together with a real voice for local communities, is essential to the management of an industry that has for too long suffered from fractured direction 128¶ and unmitigated self-interest.

In many ways, shortcomings in fisheries management on the west coast have paralleled those in forestry. The communities of Clayoquot Sound have seen their fisheries resources managed largely for the benefit of outside interests, to their own detriment. Governmental policies supporting the sustainability of stocks and habitat have too often been rendered ineffective by sophisticated harvesting technologies, industry lobbying, a dearth of knowledge about marine ecosystems, an absence of cooperation among government agencies, and lack of political will. Community voices representing a diversity of legitimate interests in fisheries management have too often gone 129¶ unheard or ignored.

The integrated, comprehensive and inclusive approach that has begun to characterize forestry management during the last few years has been missing in ocean management. The province's proposed fisheries renewal strategy, which focuses on a community-based approach to fisheries management, offers considerable hope in remedying that omission, and could play a more useful role still as a bridge towards a broader strategy with a focus beyond single resources. The fractured approach to fisheries management is a microcosm of the lack of a unified focus in coastal

management generally, with more than 30 provincial and federal agencies exercising
130¶ mandates that often conflict.

The economies of ocean-based communities like those of Clayoquot Sound have consistently suffered through decades of upland-based, forestry-focused planning in BC. The need for a coastal management strategy that coordinates governmental

---

INVITING THE SALMON HOME: THE KENNEDY LAKE SOCKEYE PROJECT

Kennedy Lake once supported a large sockeye population that sustained an aboriginal food fishery for generations and a commercial fishery for many decades. Earlier this century, about 85,000 sockeye returned from the ocean to spawn each year, but in the 1960s the sockeye population crashed. In spite of a discontinuance of commercial fishing, the stocks remained low. In 1982, the Tla-o-qui-aht people ceased their food fishery. There were still no signs of recovery, and in 1994 only 2,000 to 3,000 fish returned to spawn.[1]

In 1991, the Tla-o-qui-aht decided to invite other groups to work with them to restore the natural productivity of the lake. The result was the formation of the Kennedy Lake Technical Working Group, a joint initiative of the Tla-o-qui-aht, Ecotrust, the Department of Fisheries and Oceans, the Ministry of Forests, MacMillan Bloedel, ESSA Technologies, and local environmental and fishing groups. The working group decided to try to integrate traditional and current knowledge of the Kennedy system to create an understanding of how its natural productivity functioned, why it failed, and how it could be restored. Research has involved analysis of historical and contemporary data; field work to determine levels of spawning and smolt production, map key habitat areas, and assess the relative importance of factors affecting the sockeye population; and building a computer simulation model to integrate knowledge and explore hypotheses.

The study has yielded some unexpected findings. While commercial fishing and logging appear to have been the main causes of the precipitous decline in sockeye runs, other factors play a part in discouraging their recovery. Predation by seals, the troll fishery, poaching, and mortality at sea all have minor impacts on sockeye numbers. Yet the most likely obstacle in the way of the recovery of sockeye stocks may well be a tiny fish called the three-spined stickleback, which both preys on sockeye smolts and competes with them for habitat. When

sockeye were abundant, competition with the stickleback may not have been a serious problem, but it has become one now that stickleback outnumber juvenile sockeye by a ratio of five or ten to one. The next stage of the Kennedy Lake project is to better understand the relationship between the two species in order to explore ways in which a balance favourable to the survival of sockeye might be achieved.

The Kennedy Lake project illustrates the magnitude of the task in restoring depleted salmon stocks. Not only do we lack precise knowledge about the initial causes of stock depletion, but an understanding of what is needed for stock recovery is equally complex. There are currently at least 3,000 genetically distinct salmon stocks on the coast of BC, and probably many more.[2] The factors affecting the survival rate of one stock may be entirely different from those affecting other, for each stream is a different ecosystem, and each stock follows a different route in its ocean life cycle. In the Kennedy system, interaction with the stickleback may be the chief challenge to sockeye recovery, but in a thousand rivers and streams there are a myriad ecological interactions of which we still have little understanding.

The project also illustrates two important points that are crucial to effective conservation. First, in attempting to understand conservation needs in any given location, the detailed local knowledge that can only be gained through close examination and the experience that comes with familiarity is invaluable. And, second, cooperation among groups that can share their knowledge and understanding rather than using them for competitive purposes is the surest way to arrive at conservation solutions from which they all benefit. The trust built through the Kennedy Lake Technical Working Group may provide a useful foundation for other conservation and economic development efforts.

---

[1] *Inviting the Salmon Home: The Kennedy Lake Sockeye Project, Progress Report.* Ecotrust Canada, Tla-o-qui-aht First Nations (Vancouver and Tofino, 1995), 5.

[2] World Fisheries Trust, *The Salmon Survival Guide* (Victoria, 1995).

Community tenures are central to the recovery of BC's fisheries, and coastal communities.

actions and for coastal management plans that bring a consensus- and community-based approach to the development of opportunities and protection of marine ecosystems has long been identified and never acted on. BC lags far behind several other jurisdictions in its failure to take a comprehensive approach to coastal management issues. A carefully developed coastal management strategy would do much to lift the stagnation that currently hampers the economy of Clayoquot Sound. 131¶

Aquaculture—Conflict and Complexity

A decade ago, a salmon ordered in a restaurant would almost certainly have come from wild stocks. Since then, there has been a gradual decline in wild salmon stocks, especially high-value species. Today, as a result of the boom in fish-farming on the BC coast since the early 1980s, a large proportion of restaurant salmon are raised from hatchery eggs, are fed fish-meal pellets, and spend their lives in net pens suspended 132¶ in the ocean.

The 22 salmon farms currently licensed in Clayoquot Sound are clustered in Tofino Inlet, outer Bedwell Sound, and Fortune Channel. From a distance, the walkways that enclose the pens, close to the shoreline, look like large docks. At any given time, a few farms lie fallow during the time between the removal of mature salmon and the 133¶ introduction of a new batch of smolts.

The salmon farming industry in Clayoquot Sound supports roughly 200 full-time direct jobs and produces a quarter of BC's production of farmed fish.[36] Provincially, farmed salmon exceeded the value of the commercial wild catch in 1995, and have become BC's largest agri-food export.[37] Eighty-five per cent of the market is in the United States and Japan, and the demand continues to grow steadily, bolstered by the attractiveness to restaurants of a product that is predictably fresh, of a consistent size, and available through most of the year. Encouraged by its success to date, the industry is conducting research into the potential for farming other species such as halibut and black cod. While there are a few locally-owned farms, the dominant players in the industry are large companies, including trans-nationals based in Scandinavia, that 134¶ run the hatcheries, farm sites, processing plants and distribution systems.

Clayoquot Sound is one of the best locations on the coast for fish farming. The several large inlets in the Sound offer protected waters and lengthy shorelines that allow the farms to be widely dispersed. The water is pure and cool, its salinity is ideal, and strong tidal flows assist the dispersal of waste food and sewage. Despite these apparent advantages, the industry is the subject of a stinging controversy that places its very future in doubt. The dispute about the environmental implications of fish-farming is

[36] Marcel Gijssen, BC Salmon Farmers Association, personal communication.

[37] BC Salmon Farmers Association, *Net Work Quick Facts* (1996).

[38] *New York Times*, 1 October 1996.

[39] Ed Donaldson, Department of Fisheries and Oceans, personal communication.

[40] Ibid.

[41] Brian Harvey, World Fisheries Trust, personal communication.

every bit as polarized—and as complex—as the conflict over forestry. Accusations and counter-accusations fly back and forth between the industry and its critics, and the general public, as in the forestry debate, struggles to decide who and what to believe. For many of the questions being raised, even scientists in the field lack definitive answers. Four of the most significant concerns among many that have been raised are the potential impact of escaped salmon on wild populations, the spread of disease, degradation of the marine environment by waste from fish farms, and visual impact on the seascape.

Hybridization. Farmed fish can escape into the ocean through inadvertent release during transport or through storm and predator damage to nets. Cultured salmon include both Pacific chinook and Atlantic salmon, the latter introduced from Europe as domesticated strains known for their hardiness and rapid rate of growth. Significant numbers of Atlantic salmon have ended up in the nets of the commercial fishing industry in recent years, and escaped Atlantics have also been spotted in a number of spawning streams. Consequently, concerns have been raised about the possibility of farmed salmon interbreeding with wild stocks as well as competing with them for spawning habitat.

Attempts to establish Atlantic salmon in spawning streams years ago, when they were considered a desirable addition for the sports fishery, proved unsuccessful. A recent study found that more than 25 per cent of Atlantic salmon spawning in Norwegian streams were escapees from fish farms.[38] Atlantics in Pacific waters may be less likely to succeed at spawning because of their requirements for certain water temperatures, water velocities, sizes of gravel, food for fry and the many other conditions that species adapt to in their native habitat. Nevertheless, there remains a legitimate fear that Atlantic salmon may yet establish themselves in the wild or disrupt the spawning activity of wild stocks by their presence. Studies are currently underway to determine the biological and economic feasibility of farming monosex female or sterile Atlantic salmon, thus potentially minimizing or eliminating the possibility of reproductive interaction with wild salmon and preventing the establishment of feral populations of Atlantic salmon.[39]

Escaped farmed chinooks—the predominant species raised at Clayoquot Sound—can more easily contaminate the wild gene pool by breeding with wild stocks, as they, unlike Atlantics, are naturally adapted to west coast conditions. However, as all farmed chinooks in Clayoquot Sound are female, interbreeding can only occur through mating with wild males, as a result of which the effect of any alteration of wild gene pools would diminish over time.[40]

Diseases. Gene contamination is only one of many legitimate fears that have been raised about potential threats to wild populations from farmed fish. The stress of being enclosed in net pens greatly increases the susceptibility of farmed fish to a variety of parasites and diseases such as bacterial kidney disease and furuncolosis. Although most of the disease-causing organisms in farmed fish are also detectable in wild, healthy fish of the same species,[41] and studies in progress by scientists at the Pacific Biological Station suggest that the likelihood of disease transfer from farmed to wild stocks is remote,[42] the risk of infection remains a grave concern in an area such as Clayoquot Sound where numbers of wild stocks returning to spawn have been severely diminished by fishing pressure for several decades. 139¶

The drugs used to contain the spread of disease and parasites in farmed fish also raise concerns both about the effect on the health of the fish-farm workers who handle them and about their dispersal into the marine environment.[43] However the introduction of effective vaccines for several diseases has led to a dramatic decline in the use of antibiotics.[44] 140¶

Waste. The drugs used to control disease form one component of the waste that filters from fish farms to the marine environment. Unlike many other farm-raised species in the world, salmon are carnivorous. It takes an estimated one pound of fish meal, reduced from whole fish caught in the South American fishery, to produce a pound and a half of farmed salmon.[45] Uneaten feed combines with fish faeces and traces of drugs to produce significant amounts of waste, whose cumulative effect on marine ecosystems remains uncertain. Research is underway to reduce nitrogen and phosphorous excretion by modifying the diet of farmed salmon. While the flushing action of tidal movements can help minimize the effects of pollution, and the fallowing of farms between the removal of mature salmon and the introduction of new smolts provides a period for natural cleansing to occur, little is known about the effectiveness of fallowing[46] and tidal movements in cleansing marine ecoystems of fish-farm waste. 141¶

Aesthetics. Many residents of the Sound resent the visual intrusion of salmon farms in a wilderness setting where there is no other development. From a distance, the farms loom large to kayakers and other boaters drawn to the waters of the sound by the prospect of undisturbed wilderness. Wilderness may well be the tourism industry's greatest asset in the future, and as that industry develops, the potential for conflict with the salmon farming industry will continue to exist. Ultimately, relocation of those salmon-farms that are currently located in otherwise pristine areas such as Sydney and Shelter inlets may be the only way of preserving important wilderness values. 142¶

Like the forest industry earlier in the century, salmon-farming arrived in British Columbia in the 1980s with the intensity of a gold rush, with little initial regulation or understanding of its impacts on local ecosystems. And, as with forestry, the tendency during the early years of the industry was to treat concerns about potential environmental impacts too lightly. Far less is known about the interactions of marine species than about those of terrestrial species. Several of the environmental risks of salmon-farming—particularly the likelihood and genetic effects of intra- and inter-specific breeding—have not yet been closely researched by the scientific community. 143¶

Wild salmon stocks are far too important to the economy and culture of the west coast to be exposed to unknown risks in addition to those that have already placed them in jeopardy. Society cannot afford the risk of repeating the mistakes so often made in BC's history of resource exploitation—ignoring ecological consequences of industrial activity for the sake of short-term gain, often with catastrophic results.

[42] Trevor Evelyn, Department of Fisheries and Oceans, Pacific Biological Station, personal communication.

[43] David W. Ellis and Associates, *Net Loss: The Salmon Netcage Industry in British Columbia* (Vancouver: David Suzuki Foundation, 1996), 114-15.

[44] Trevor Evelyn, personal communication.

[45] Ellis and Associates, op. cit., 91.

[46] Environmental Assessment Office, Salmon Aquaculture Review, *Response to Public Comment on Proposed Review Process and Draft Terms of Reference* (Victoria, 1996).

Caution in condoning an industry whose environmental impacts are not fully known
144¶ is essential.

In 1992, in response to public concerns about fish farming, the BC government
placed a moratorium on the issuance of new licences, and three years later announced
both a policy review and an environmental impact review by the Environmental
Assessment Office, to be completed in early 1997. If the very serious concerns about
the risk of hybridization are found to be justified, a requirement for farmed salmon to
be sterile or of a single sex should be considered to ensure protection of the genetic
integrity of wild stocks. And if concerns about the likelihood and effects of disease
transfer and about the impacts of fish-farm waste on marine ecosystems cannot be
satisfactorily addressed, complete enclosure of fish-farming operations, using bags
145¶ with water filtration systems, should be contemplated.

Shellfish Farming—An Ideal Fit

The clean, nutrient-rich waters and broad intertidal areas of Clayoquot Sound support an abundance of clams, oysters, scallops, sea urchins, geoducks, and Dungeness
crabs. In addition to native species, the large Japanese oysters and Manila clams
became well established several decades ago. Species that have suffered significant
declines because of overharvesting include abalone, which was closed to fishing several years ago, and the giant geoduck, a clam
which has been taken in large quantities by divers
and, because of its longevity, is slow to reproduce
146¶ and therefore extremely vulnerable to depletion.

Shellfish farming is a relatively new and rapidly
growing industry in Clayoquot Sound. Under
licences of occupation issued by the provincial
government, Pacific oysters and Manila clams are
cultivated on intertidal beaches. In addition,
both species and Pacific scallops are grown on
lines suspended in deeper waters. The concept is
disarmingly simple. Lines seeded with juveniles
(spat) are lowered into protected waters, where
they grow to maturity and are harvested eighteen
months to two years later. Lemmens Inlet has
been found to produce the fastest-growing farmed
147¶ oysters in BC.

There are currently 11 licences for shellfish farms
in Clayoquot Sound, operated primarily by companies based on the east coast of Vancouver
Island and in Vancouver. The primary constraint
on the expansion of the industry at present is
unresolved First Nations land claims, which
reduce the availability of beach tenures. Land
access is needed not only for beach culture but

The shift is back to an economy of abundance
based on the richness of the sea, the tidelands, the
rivers and—to a much lesser degree—the forests.

for deepwater operations, which must place harvested shellfish on beaches for a period in order to harden their shells and increase their shelf life. 148¶

Formerly, licences of occupation could be awarded to local growers without competition. Now, in consultation with the shellfish industry, the Ministry of Environment, Lands and Parks selects new sites (generally from previously abandoned licences of occupation) and puts them up for public auction.[47] The new system, put in place to ensure maximum revenue to the public purse, is a source of chagrin to local people who are unable to compete with the superior financial resources of the larger companies in the industry. 149¶

The absence of local processing facilities means that shellfish in a Tofino restaurant, for example, may have been harvested in Clayoquot Sound, shipped across Vancouver Island, processed and inspected, then shipped back to Tofino before being made available for consumption. The development of local processing operations

[47] Doug Berry, Lands Officer, Ministry of Environment Lands and Parks, personal communication.

[48] Brian Kingzett, President, BC Shellfish Growers Association, personal communication.

THE LEGACY OF THE SEA OTTER
By David Greer

At the end of the eighteenth century, the pelt of the sea otter was one of the most highly prized furs in the world. In four decades, from 1780 to 1820, European and American hunters—with the aid of Native people on the coast—virtually eliminated the sea otter from BC waters. The sea urchin was a significant part of the otter's diet, and when the otter disappeared, sea urchin populations multiplied. They in turn, grazing on seaweed, gradually destroyed the kelp forests along the outer coast.

Kelp beds provide the basis for complex biological communities. For a variety of fish species, kelp provides not only feeding and spawning grounds but also protection from predators. By limiting the effects of wave action, kelp also moderates the effects of erosion.

Between 1969 and 1972, the federal government began reintroducing the sea otter to BC waters. It transplanted a small colony of 85 animals from Alaska to the Bunsby Islands, off Vancouver Island's northwest coast. By the early 1990s, the sea otter population on the BC coast had grown to 800. Today there are reports of kelp forests again returning to parts of the coast.

Each of the multitude of plant and animal species in an ecosystem makes a contribution, through predator-prey relationships and other interactions, to keeping the ecosystem in balance. Removal of a single species can set off a chain reaction that disrupts the entire ecosystem. The sea otter is a "keystone" species—one whose removal, like the keystone in an arch, affects the stability of the whole structure. The significance of many other species in maintaining the balance of both marine and terrestrial ecosystems is little understood. However, the destruction of the sea otter reveals how great the consequences, both ecological and economic, can be when humans ignore or fail to understand the chain-reaction effect that may occur when they deplete a species that is perceived simply as an economic resource and nothing more. It also illustrates that we cannot effectively assess the impact of an economic activity on the sustainability of an ecosystem in the absence of a comprehensive knowledge of the dynamics of that ecosystem.

The introduction of an exotic species into an ecosystem can be as disruptive as the removal of a native species. The survival mechanisms that creatures develop through eons of evolution are effective for the ecosystem in which they exist, but may be wholly inadequate against species introduced from other ecosystems. The farming of Atlantic salmon and of hatchery-raised Pacifics in aquaculture operations has raised legitimate concerns about the potential impact of escaped farm fish mingling with wild populations in the ocean and in spawning streams. Proponents of the use of Atlantics argue that there is little evidence of actual risk from disease, predation, or competition for spawning areas. But, as has so often been learned too late in the past, placing a native species at risk is a poor way to answer such questions. In an ecosystem, as in medicine, the guiding principle should be, "First, do no harm."

may be impeded both by an absence of available foreshore and by a shortage of fresh water supplies, although shellfish processing requires significantly less water than does fish-processing. A larger industry, with greater local participation, would 150¶ enhance the feasibility of developing local processing facilities.

The shellfish industry provides one of the best opportunities for increased local employment in Clayoquot Sound. In a few other coastal areas the industry has rapidly become either the major or one of the largest employers, with a 1995 BC-wide farm gate value for oysters, clams and scallops of more than $9 million. The market for shucked and whole shellfish has remained consistently strong and is growing rapidly, with opportunities for further expansion in California, Hong Kong, Taiwan, and possibly mainland China. In addition to existing production of scallops, oysters and clams, there is significant potential in the local mariculture industry for expan- 151¶ sion to include geoducks, abalone, sea urchins, sea cucumbers, and kelp.[48]

Few of the environmental concerns about salmon-farming apply to the shellfish-farming industry, and the conditions needed for the industry—large intertidal areas, protected deepwater areas, and water temperature, flow and salinity—are virtually ideal in Clayoquot Sound. The risk of pollution of shellfish-growing areas is primar- ily from boating—oil and diesel spills, sewage discharge from pleasure boats, and copper- and tin-based antifoulants—but is far less than other areas of the coast where 152¶ septic seepage has caused industry shutdowns.

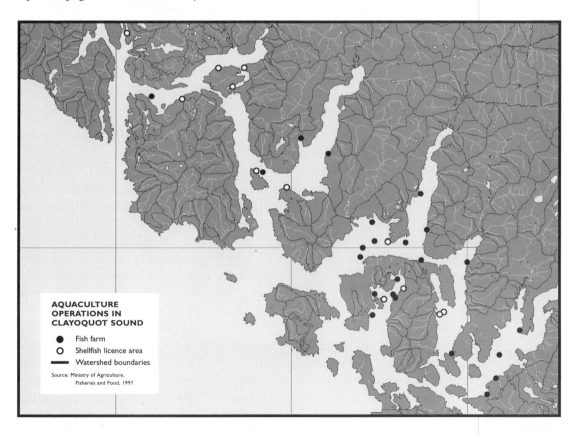

AQUACULTURE OPERATIONS IN CLAYOQUOT SOUND
● Fish farm
○ Shellfish licence area
— Watershed boundaries
Source: Ministry of Agriculture, Fisheries and Food, 1997

Tours of remote areas of Clayoquot Sound by kayak, provided by local businesses, are in high demand.

One of the biggest challenges will be to increase the opportunity for local involvement in the industry, which is currently dominated by companies based on the east coast of Vancouver Island and in Vancouver. Obtaining the highest dollar value from licences is a false economy if it fails to factor in benefits to the community, both in direct and indirect employment, of local participation. A practical way of increasing those benefits would be through the creation of community tenures. Under this arrangement, an area of the Sound would be given over to a local group for management, with growing rights being granted to individuals by the community. In addition to ensuring greater economic benefit to the community, such a system has the potential to reduce both the administrative burden of government and avoid the lengthy time currently required for licence applications to pass through the referral process. Proposals for policy changes to enable community tenures to exist are at an early stage of discussion within government[49] and should be encouraged. 153¶

Tourism—In the Eye of the Beholder

More than half a million tourists visit Clayoquot Sound every year, and about half of those visitors come from outside British Columbia.[50] While Pacific Rim National Park draws the great majority of visitors, the publicity generated by the conflict over forest practices has resulted in an increased interest, nationally and in other parts of the world, in other areas of Clayoquot Sound as a tourist destination. The number of visitors to the Tofino tourist information centre increased by roughly 18 per cent annually between the late 1980s and mid 1990s. Whale-watching—for migrant and resident grays as well as the occasional appearance of orcas—has become hugely popular in recent years. In the spring and fall, birders are treated to the spectacle of hundreds of thousands of migrating shorebirds congregating at the Tofino mudflats and on the outer coast beaches. Tours of remote areas of Clayoquot Sound by kayak, provided by local businesses, are in high demand. A trail through the old-growth forest of Meares Island has been so heavily used that a boardwalk was built to protect the roots of giant cedars, and the recently completed Wild Side Heritage Trail on Flores Island, complete with campsites, has gained instant popularity. 154¶

[49] Michael Coon, Ministry of Agriculture, Fisheries and Food, personal communication.

[50] Parks Canada, *Long Beach Exit Survey,* 1994, v.

[51] *Tofino Community Values Survey,* 1991.

Each of these activities hints at the future direction for tourism in Clayoquot Sound—one that focuses on the natural scenic values of ocean and rain forest and avoids excessive development. The addition of new parks through the Clayoquot Sound land use decision creates enormous potential for trails across a variety of landscapes. Some routes, like the trail that runs from the head of Bedwell Sound to the alpine areas of Strathcona Park, will likely cross both protected areas and publicly owned forest lands. Perhaps the future will see a northward extension of the West Coast Trail that, with the recent creation of the Juan de Fuca extension, now runs from Jordan River north to Barkley Sound. There is potential as well for wilderness lodges, privately operated on Crown land, that will not only provide accommodation but also serve as bases for wilderness-oriented recreation.

155¶

There is enormous potential for hiking trails across a variety of landscapes in Clayoquot Sound.

Natural history and cultural heritage are both themes that can usefully be developed as the tourist industry continues to evolve. Whales and old-growth trees are naturally inspiring because of their size. The subtle diversity of marine and forest habitats can be equally fascinating if presented to tourists in ways that they can be understood and appreciated, as demonstrated by the interpretive programs that have been so successful at Pacific Rim National Park. As well, cultural interpretive programs could be developed to encourage an understanding and appreciation of past and present First Nations ways of life and the shared history and culture since Europeans and Asians arrived on the west coast. Such programs might include tours of ancient cedars modified by early aboriginal use, along with demonstrations of traditional uses of cedar; and displays and interpretations that reveal the evolution of resource uses from the early days of the Nuu-chah-nulth to the present day.

156¶

A community values survey conducted in Tofino confirmed that local residents want to see an emphasis on less intensive, locally controlled tourism activities with a focus on the natural and cultural values of Clayoquot Sound. The types of development that received the highest level of approval included the following: bike paths, tourism that promotes environmental awareness, tourism developments by local residents rather than outsiders, small rather than large developments, hiking trails, cultural activities, and tourist wilderness experiences. On the other end of the scale, developments that attracted the least support included trophy hunting, more whale-watching tours, pubs, sport-fishing charters, concession stands on beaches, hotels, motels and restaurants.[51]

157¶

The expansion of the tourist industry has not come without a price. During the winter, Tofino preserves much of the character of a quiet fishing village; in the summer its streets swarm with tourists and parking spaces in the centre of town are often unobtainable. The community values survey found that most residents felt significantly inconvenienced by the crowding and congestion caused by summer tourists. As a result of the ongoing conversion of dozens of homes to bed-and-breakfast facilities, permanent and seasonal residents alike struggle to find accommodation and pay an inflated price if they are successful. Competition for limited boat docking space increases year by year. If the tourist industry is to continue to expand, its impact on 158¶ Tofino will need to be carefully managed.

The foundation for planning further tourism development in Clayoquot Sound is currently being laid by the interagency team charged with implementing the recommendations of the scientific panel. Once the team has completed inventories of tourism and recreation values, a planning process will be developed in conjunction with the Central Region Board and those with a direct interest in the tourist industry.[52] There is little doubt that whatever process emerges will face significant challenges in resolving conflicts that already exist among proponents of different philosophies of development, and in ensuring that proposed developments are not 159¶ likely to damage marine or terrestrial environments.

The combination of natural beauty, wildness and accessibility in Clayoquot Sound is unmatched by any other area in North America. As the demand among urban populations for access to beautiful and unspoiled environments inevitably continues to expand, the appeal of Clayoquot Sound as a tourist destination will grow as well. The tourist industry has tremendous potential as a major component of a diversified economy that is conservation-based, provided its direction is carefully guided in a 160¶ manner that respects the wishes of local residents.

Forestry—A Future Rooted in Communities

The forest industry has been the mainstay of economic growth in BC for most of the twentieth century. Yet, in the ratio of jobs created to the amount of timber cut, the industry has been in decline for decades. The tree farm licence system of tenures was brought in during the late 1940s in response to decades of criticism that temporary tenures encouraged a cut-and-run philosophy among forest companies. By providing a guarantee of renewable tenures on fixed areas of forest, TFLs were intended to ensure sustainable management of forest resources. However, they soon proved inadequate in providing sustainable levels of either timber supplies or employment among forest workers. More efficient harvesting technologies introduced in the 1950s and later decades led inevitably to higher harvest volumes and a less labour-intensive industry. Later, sales of fast-growing fibre in tropical and subtropical regions forced the BC industry to automate its operations as much as possible to remain competitive. This led to further reductions in the size of the labour force in forestry dependent communities throughout the province. During the 1980s, the number of jobs produced per thousand cubic metres of timber on the BC coast dropped from 1.7 to 1.3, and employment in the forest industry fell by over 25 per cent, despite rela- 161¶ tively constant harvest volumes.[53]

The effect in the Alberni-Clayoquot Regional District was even greater. Job loss in the forest industry was the major contributor to a net out-migration of 6.8 per cent in the regional district between 1981 and 1986. Cutbacks in the workforce at MacMillan

[52] Pieter Bekker, Ministry of Small Business, Tourism and Culture, personal communication.

[53] Commission on Resources and Environment, *Vancouver Island Land Use Plan* (Victoria, 1994), 44-45.

[54] Ministry of Government Services (BC Stats), *British Columbia Regional Index*, 1995, 39.

[55] Herb Hammond, *Seeing the Forest Among the Trees: The Case for Wholistic Forest Use* (Winlaw, BC: Polestar Press, 1991), 78-80.

Bloedel's Kennedy Lake division were devastating for Ucluelet, where forestry had been the major employer in the early 1980s. By 1995, only 9 per cent of Ucluelet's workers were employed in forestry related jobs. In Port Alberni, the closure of two mills in 1991 resulted in a loss of 480 jobs. In a little more than a decade, the number of workers employed in the forest industry in the regional district has fallen by 50 per cent.[54]

162¶

The Forest Practices Code, which became law in 1995, simply provided clout to a legal obligation that had already long existed—to sustain timber supplies and ensure the care of non-timber values in the management of the province's forests—but had been exercised less than rigorously. Together with a reduction in permitted volumes of cut to encourage sustainable timber supplies, the code has further eroded employment levels in the harvesting and primary processing of timber throughout the province. In Clayoquot Sound, the more stringent standards demanded by the scientific panel will have an additional, and still undetermined, long-term effect on traditional types of harvesting and processing jobs in the forest industry.

163¶

As part of a new strategy to create employment for displaced forestry workers, the BC government in 1994 introduced the Forest Renewal Plan. Funded through stumpage revenues (taxes on harvested timber), Forest Renewal BC is meant to complement the Forest Practices Code by working towards the restoration of ecosystems damaged by past logging practices and to restore logged-over lands to productive timber use. Funds from the plan are being used for spacing, pruning and thinning of second growth forests; reducing the risk of erosion and landslides by deactivating old logging roads and restoring salmon-bearing streams damaged by logging; and retraining forest workers for these activities and new careers. In Clayoquot Sound, Forest Renewal BC currently funds ecosystem inventories needed for the implementation of scientific panel recommendations, and supports a skills training centre in Ucluelet.

164¶

The Forest Renewal Plan has been a stopgap measure in a jobs creation strategy designed to assist displaced forest workers. In the future, however, the health of the local forest industry will depend on the ability to produce jobs in small-scale forestry that derives maximum value from the timber used and creates local employment. Current governmental programs and institutional structures do not readily encourage such a transition. Ninety per cent of forest land in Clayoquot Sound remains locked in the two tree farm licences managed by MacMillan Bloedel and International Forest Products (Interfor), which holds the licence originally granted to BC Forest Products. The value to local communities created by the forests under the control of these companies is largely limited to the jobs created by timber harvesting operations. Once logged, Clayoquot Sound timber is shipped elsewhere—primarily Port Alberni and Vancouver—for processing into paper and lumber, which in turn are exported for remanufacturing.

165¶

Value-added manufacturing can create several times the number of jobs created by primary processing. A 1991 study estimated that the US creates 3.5 jobs for every one created by the same volume of timber in BC.[55] Currently, about 40 people in the Ucluelet area and 20 in Tofino are involved either full- or part-time in small manufacturing operations whose products include cedar shakes, furniture, cabinetry, trim,

Wood supply shortages are only one of several obstacles that value-added operators must overcome to establish a successful operation.

guitar tops, carvings, and custom-cut lumber.[56] However, the number of these operations has declined in recent years, primarily as a result of timber shortages. In past years, the primary source of supply has been waste timber salvaged from the operations of tree farm licensees. But the supply of salvage wood has been blocked by an unwillingness by major licence holders to free up wood, high stumpage rates, and tougher new forest practices standards. In compliance with those standards, tree farm licensees have deactivated poorly built forestry roads that once provided access to salvage sites. Moreover, salvage wood will be in increasingly short supply in the future as licensees comply with new requirements to minimize timber waste.

Future opportunities for value-added operators will depend increasingly on their ability to obtain access to standing timber and to purchase logs from forest companies. The BC government has announced but has not yet implemented a program to provide credits to tree farm licensees that make logs available to value-added businesses. A Ministry of Forests pilot project to provide direct award timber sales is in the beginning stages. Timber may also be made available through the development of woodlots—forested areas that are made available by the Ministry of Forests for long-term management by small holders—but these will remain unavailable until planning in accordance with the scientific panel recommendations is undertaken.[57]

In the longer term, carefully managed community forests could provide the most practical means of ensuring long-term timber supplies to Clayoquot Sound businesses. Under this arrangement, the Ministry of Forests makes areas available for forest management by a community, which pays stumpage on harvested timber and guarantees timber availability to local operators. The Nuu-chah-nulth First Nations are considering the establishment of community forests for their people. The challenge in a community like Tofino may lie in securing the broad level of public support needed for any arrangement that involves timber harvesting in the rain forest.

Wood supply shortages are only one of several obstacles that value-added operators must overcome to establish a successful operation. Traditional lenders are reluctant to provide financing to businesses with uncertain wood supplies and, in some cases, uncertain markets. Value-added businesses are often unable to obtain access to the industrial sites needed for storing and drying wood and for conducting manufacturing operations. Businesses that succeed in obtaining access to timber must now be prepared for the additional expense of locating and protecting culturally modified trees and medicinal plants, an essential requirement for the protection of First Nations cultural history.

Finally, such businesses must cope with the perception that small value-added operations are a sideline in an industry that for decades has focused on the export of raw logs and lumber. Indeed, the whole structure of the market makes it difficult to connect

[56]Patricia Greer, *Value-Added Wood Products Report,* prepared for the people and communities of the Long Beach Model Forest (December 1995).

[57]Paul Pashnik, District Manager, Port Alberni Forest District, personal communication.

[58]Ken Drushka, Bob Nixon and Ray Travers, eds., *Touch Wood: BC Forests at the Crossroads* (Madeira Park; Harbour Publishing, 1993), 6.

small-scale harvesting operations with buyers and processors. Yet the economic stability of Clayoquot Sound communities in the future will depend on their ability to derive as much value as possible from local timber resources.

The announcement of the Clayoquot Sound land use decision was accompanied by a commitment by the BC government to actively promote value-added manufacturing in local communities. The government is gradually taking steps to make good its promise, but a stronger commitment will be needed to reverse the fortunes of a stagnating industry, caught between new forest practice standards and an outdated tenure system that undermines local economies.

The existing tree farm licence system was devised in the 1940s as a means of ensuring sustainable timber productivity. As originally conceived, TFLs were to be divided among hundreds of small companies; instead, they fell into the hands of a few large corporations which obtained them as a windfall for no cost[58] and generally failed to sustain either timber supplies or ecosystem integrity. For several reasons, the time has come to rethink the tenure system as it applies to Clayoquot Sound. Tree farm licences were put into place at a time when forests were considered of economic value only for the timber they produced and when it was deemed desirable to promote rapid economic growth narrowly focused on large-scale industrial production. Today it has become clear that the future well-being of communities such as Clayoquot Sound will depend on their ability to develop diverse, small-scale economies that derive maximum local value from natural resources. As an institutional arrangement that reflects a contrary purpose, the tree farm licence system not only is no longer relevant to current needs but stands in the way of their fulfilment. In recognition of the need to ensure the best public use of Clayoquot Sound forests, and to create opportunities for small-scale forestry through alternatives such as community forests, the government should give serious consideration to terminating tree farm licences in the region. The government has consistently rejected proposals to reform the forest land tenure system, yet it is becoming increasingly clear that such reform is essential if communities like those in Clayoquot Sound are to develop local forest industries that are both economically and ecologically sound.

Education—Clayoquot Sound's New Growth Industry

Till now, fishing, forestry and tourism have been considered the major economic opportunities open to rural coastal communities in general and Tofino in particular. These occupations represent mature industries that have proven value and a certain historic resonance in Tofino. Each will assuredly survive, although in the case of forestry in a much diminished form. Each will change over time, and each will be a base for spin-off operations that add value to the basic raw materials. But fishing and forestry have entered a period of declining economic importance. And tourism does not generate the big boom or bust salaries of the resource extraction industries and has the disadvantage of abrupt seasonality.

A fourth area upon which a healthy local community can be based is education. Small communities generally consider education as an expense, but there are many towns, villages and small cities that have welcomed, encouraged and nurtured educational organizations to the point where they have become major pillars of economic activity. Tofino has begun the process of creating a network of educational and research institutions that might actually develop into the economic backbone of the town. 174¶

Indeed, Clayoquot Sound has the opportunity to become a globally important centre for coastal ecosystem studies. It is remote but accessible. It combines forest and marine ecosystems with a complex coastal interface. It contrasts thousands of years of native interaction with the ecosystem with 200 years of European impact. It demonstrates various methods of resource management. It offers a multitude of opportunities to study the functions of the coastal temperate rain forest. Clayoquot Sound will probably be designated as a United Nations Man and the Biosphere Reserve, and as such will receive further international attention, becoming a magnet for research activities. The communities of Clayoquot Sound, rather than the educa- 175¶ tion centres of Victoria or Vancouver, should become the location of this activity.

The seeds of an education economy are already sown through the activities of the Clayoquot Biosphere Project, the School for Field Studies (currently operating at Bamfield in Barkley Sound) and Long Beach Model Forest. The Biosphere Project in particular has already signalled a desire to expand its network of field stations to include classrooms and a laboratory, and to build closer links with outside academic 176¶ institutions through its proposed Clayoquot Centre for Coastal Studies.

There are several models for the kinds of institutions that could develop in Clayoquot Sound. One is the Organization for Tropical Studies. This organization is based at Duke University in the US and represents a consortium of more than 60 universities. Each pays annual dues of about $12,000 US. This money goes to support an administrative infrastructure as well as three field stations in Costa Rica. Students from the member schools are then eligible to attend courses and participate in both short- and long-term research projects to do with tropical biology. Courses range from two-week introductions to tropical biology, agroforestry and sustainable agriculture to full semester credit courses in a broad range of ecosystem topics. Graduate students incorporate six-month to two-year research efforts at the OTS field stations in degree 177¶ programs at their home university.

Another example Tofino can look to is the Woods Hole Oceanographic Institution at Woods Hole, Massachusetts. Until the 1940s, Woods Hole was a small town on Cape Cod with an economy based on commercial fishing and a small amount of tourism. At present the research and educational activities of several independent but cooperative institutions comprise the major economic activity of the town. Both Harvard and the Massachusetts Institute of Technology have joint degree-granting programs, and vanguard research in oceanography, climatology and fisheries is conducted at Woods Hole. Ancillary institutions have developed there, offering programs ranging from 178¶ high school research internships through post doctoral fellowships.

Education as an industry or economic sector offers many benefits to a community. Unlike most tourism, fishing and forestry operations, it is not just a seasonal activity. Direct and indirect spending and activity is spread out over the whole year. The jobs created are not only those of faculty and administration, but involve a range of support roles involved in housing, meals, construction, maintenance, and field study guides. The impact on local business would be highly supportive. Researchers buy gas, groceries, tools, and various equipment. Students eat at restaurants and shop locally. Their parents come to visit. In addition to the economic benefits, there would be positive impacts in other areas. Local elementary and secondary schools would have access to a whole new set of resources. Native and non-native children would have an enriched menu of opportunities, rarely available in rural areas. To encourage further development of this sector, First Nations, the provincial government, the municipality and the regional district could demonstrate support through a proclamation of willingness to facilitate organizations wishing to become established in Clayoquot Sound. Tofino could set aside district lands in a special educational and research zone. These do not have to be donated, but rather can be offered with a package of development incentives. Other adjustments to zoning by-laws to accommodate student and faculty residences may be advisable.

RE-IMAGINING THE LANDSCAPE: TOWARDS A BIOSPHERE RESERVE
By Erin Kellogg

The peoples of Clayoquot Sound have long recognized this area of land and sea as a coherent whole. Federal and provincial agencies and even local governments may carve it into a mosaic of overlapping jurisdictions, but any serious attempts to resolve land-use conflicts have had to return to the larger tableau of the entire Clayoquot Sound watershed. For several years, scientists, conservationists, First Nations, and policymakers have entertained the idea of seeking designation of Clayoquot Sound as a UNESCO Man and the Biosphere Reserve (MAB). Such a designation could serve to solidify the region's boundaries for purposes of conservation and development planning, and at the same time help confirm its global ecological importance.

The UNESCO Man and the Biosphere program, instituted in 1976, provides a framework for re-imagining a landscape like Clayoquot Sound without adding a new layer of bureaucracy. The term "biosphere reserve" is an international designation created and awarded by UNESCO to an area which has been nominated by a MAB national committee, and which has met the selection criteria. (The Clayoquot Biosphere Project in Tofino [see page 23] has a similar name, but is not related to the UN biosphere reserve program.)

MAB designation captures the natural ecological and cultural contours of a place like Clayoquot Sound—providing an organizing framework for planning and management without mandating any prescriptive practices. A biosphere reserve has no legal jurisdiction, and is merely a tool for organizing information and people to solve problems and promote conservation and development in a regional context. MAB designation is voluntary and must be initiated and supported by local people and institutions before the national MAB secretariat will even nominate an area for UNESCO's consideration. Selection depends on local communities' understanding of the biosphere reserve concept, agreement with its goals, and commitment to long-term cooperative management. To date there are over 250 biosphere reserves in 71 countries world-wide, including six in Canada.

Biosphere reserves allow for great flexibility in both spatial arrangement and management approaches. Each reserve has three components: a core area of relatively undisturbed protected land and/or water that conserves ecological processes and functions; a buffer zone surrounding the core area that protects its ecological integrity, where activities that contribute to this protection such as research, traditional native use, and nature- and culture-based tourism occur; and a zone of cooperation where sustainable or conservation-based development activities are encouraged and supported. Some biosphere reserves have built on existing institutions and others have created new organizational structures to coordinate the range of activities in the reserve, including planning, research and monitoring, and community economic development.

The Western Canada Wilderness Committee first promoted the idea of a Clayoquot Sound biosphere reserve in its newsletters in the late 1980s, and in its 1991 book *Clayoquot on the Wild Side.* Following the provincial government's 1993 land use decision, CORE Commissioner Stephen Owen recommended that Clayoquot Sound be designated as a United Nations biosphere reserve. In its ensuing report on the Clayoquot Sound decision, which was distributed to 1.1 million households in BC, the government agreed to "vigorously pursue an International Biosphere Reserve designation for Clayoquot Sound." Shortly thereafter, the Clayoquot Biosphere Project and Ecotrust hosted a symposium to explore the feasibility of and interest in UNESCO designation for Clayoquot Sound. The symposium was attended by Canadian MAB representatives George Francis and Peter Pearse, as well as local scientists and Native and non-Native residents. At this point the Nuu-chah-nulth were negotiating the first Interim Measures Agreement with the province. It was clear that any biosphere reserve proposal would require the active leadership and support of Clayoquot's First Nations, but that before an Interim Measures Agreement was in effect, this would not be possible.

Understandably, few people in Clayoquot Sound have been ready to seek its designation as a UNESCO Man and the Biosphere Reserve. The local land-use planning processes and polarization that led to the 1993 decision left little energy and appetite for venturing into an international arena. The government, although it had voiced commitment to the idea in 1993, was reluctant to pursue designation until the findings of the scientific panel (see pages 27-28) were released and adopted. Now that the dust has settled, the scientific panel's recommendations have been accepted, the Nuu-chah-nulth have been assured an increasing degree of authority and security through the extension of the Interim Measures Agreement, and Clayoquot Sound's residents have begun building a future that manages for abundance, the time for a MAB designation may be more auspicious.

In many ways, Clayoquot Sound already embodies the best attributes of a biosphere reserve:

• the area retains much of its ecological splendor

and core protection is already afforded through Pacific Rim National Park, Strathcona Provincial Park, and the areas set aside in the 1993 decision, although the unprotected pristine watersheds should be afforded greater protection;

• it continues to provide examples of ecologically sustainable resource use through the work of the Nuu-chah-nulth First Nations, the scientific panel, the West Coast Sustainability Association and many others.

• the Clayoquot Biosphere Project, the Long Beach Model Forest, and others are actively promoting the area as a centre for research, education, training, and monitoring of natural and managed ecosystems.

• the Central Regional Board has taken a great step towards providing cooperative, comprehensive oversight of land-use management in the Sound.

The Central Region Board is now seriously exploring the potential for biosphere reserve status as a vehicle for achieving greater consensus in Clayoquot Sound and for drawing more resources to the area for innovative economic development. The provincial government has also voiced greater support for designation, and is working with environmental groups and others to agree on conditions for wholesale government support. Likewise, the federal government has voiced its support for designating Clayoquot Sound as a biosphere reserve.

MAB designation could aid in the development of an economic transition strategy to help guide a long-lasting shift to a more diversified, sustainable regional economy that will benefit all residents and workers. It could also provide a mechanism for implementing the scientific panel recommendations in a manner that ensures scientific research is undertaken with First Nations as equal partners. And MAB designation could mirror efforts on the part of the Nuu-chah-nulth to create tribal parks. Francis Frank, chief councillor of the Tla-o-qui-aht First Nations, said that while the Tla-o-qui-aht insist that Meares Island still deserves to be explicitly designated a tribal park, other tribal park proposals could be absorbed by a MAB designation.[1] For many reasons, therefore, Clayoquot Sound deserves the international recognition conferred by designation as a UNESCO Man and the Biosphere Reserve.

[1] Francis Frank, personal communication.

People, Place and Prosperity:
Clayoquot Sound in the Coming Century

BY IAN GILL AND DAVID GREER

The Path Less Travelled

The need to develop diversified, small-scale economies that do not degrade the environment or diminish its natural abundance has been readily apparent for years now, yet our economic and governmental structures stand in the way of that urgent transition. The rural communities of British Columbia have learned this all too well. Dependent on forestry or fishing, they have seen their economies suffer both through the loss of jobs to technology and through the depletion of the resources that provide those jobs in the first place. There are few options for young people raised in rural communities to be educated there and find meaningful work. Now, as these communities struggle to develop new economies and to gain a measure of control over their own economic destiny, they find themselves constrained by the entrenched regimes of the frontier economy.

For far too long, residents of coastal communities in rural British Columbia have seen their natural resources controlled and drawn away by distant corporations with little stake in maintaining the well-being of local communities or protecting local environments from the consequences of over-development. Although it has become popular for governments to support the principle of community self-sufficiency and a greater local role in resource management, coastal communities still face formidable obstacles. Marine resources continue to be sucked away to urban centres and the conglomerates that control the seafood industries. On land, the wealth of the forests—their cultural and ecological values, their recreational potential, their timber and non-timber resource wealth—exists almost as a taunt to local residents, who live surrounded by great abundance but are denied all but the most minimal access to it. The land remains firmly locked in timber tenures held for the most part by international corporations.

Meaningful support for economic development that conserves natural and cultural values must begin in places like Clayoquot Sound. The residents of those communities have a vested interest in conserving the forests and oceans that are their home—the place they look to for spiritual well-being, economic sustenance, and recreation. They neither want to exploit nor save their environment. They merely

There are few options for young people raised in rural communities to be educated there and find meaningful work.

want to live in it. Together with an inherent motivation to provide responsible stewardship, they bring an intimate knowledge of the land and sea—knowledge that can be enhanced but not duplicated by scientific knowledge or technical expertise. 182¶

In Clayoquot Sound that knowledge is particularly rich because it is rooted in several thousand years of Nuu-chah-nulth tradition. To the Nuu-chah-nulth, natural resources were regarded as gifts that must not be squandered. This notion that "everything is one" was embodied in the tradition of *hishuk ish ts'awalk.* Ownership and use rights to lands and resources were strictly defined, and the chiefs who held these rights were responsible for ensuring that the fruits of natural abundance were shared among families and com- 183¶ munities. This system was called *hahuulhi.*

In Clayoquot Sound an economy is emerging that marks a symbolic return to the original Nuu-chah-nulth approach to the management for abundance, which provides an excellent precedent for the development of a balanced, diversified economy that rewards care and respect. The argument that the Nuu-chah-nulth might have adopted a more exploitive approach to resource management if they had had different technologies and demanding markets, even if it is valid, is irrelevant. The fact remains that, both in philosophy and practice, the traditional Nuu-chah-nulth system offers an enlightening alternative to an industrial economy that has often too often undermined community and environmental stability in the name of corporate profit. 184¶

The residents of Clayoquot Sound have the knowledge and the motivation to build a diversified, conservation-based economy. They live in an area of extraordinary natural wealth. Given the proper tools to build on their knowledge—starting with a recognition of its value and importance—they have the potential to set an example to the world of a community where the principles of economic, ecological and community 185¶ sustainability are practised with success.

A great deal of groundwork has already been laid. The decade of bitter conflict over logging in Clayoquot Sound forced the government to impose its "moderate" 1993 land use plan, which utterly failed to get to the root of community concerns in the Sound. There was a visceral reaction to the plan, 800-plus arrests and widespread condemnation of the continued destruction, for corporate gain, of one of the world's most magnificent remaining temperate rain forests. The alienation was so intensely felt that 186¶ it produced—somewhat fortuitously—a climate for even more profound change.

59 Scientific Panel for Sustainable Forest Practices in Clayoquot Sound, *Report 3: First Nations' Perspectives Relating to Forest Practices Standards in Clayoquot Sound* (March 1995), 51.

The 1993 decision, like processes that preceded it, was hobbled by the constraints of industrial forestry and the tree farm licences that the industry controlled on the majority of public land. Therein lay the fundamental contradiction: at one and the same time, government promised a new economic plan for Clayoquot Sound while remaining committed to an industrial hold on the land that effectively blocked alternative economic development. Moreover, the land use decision, by definition, did not address the fundamental reality that Clayoquot Sound communities today, as always in the past, look far more to the ocean than to the land for their economic well-being.

The criticism that followed the 1993 decision sowed the seeds of a new planning order in British Columbia, as exemplified by the independent Scientific Panel for Sustainable Forest Practices in Clayoquot Sound, and the formation of the Central Region Board. Between them, the scientific panel and the CRB have produced a level of public involvement in planning unheard of a few years ago. And despite years of bruising argument and division, of international attention and a relentless media glare, exhausting years of planning and analysis and conflict and dissent, the people of Clayoquot Sound *do* still want to be involved. What those years have forged is a community of people who have the experience, the durability, the resilience, the knowledge, the ingenuity and the drive to govern themselves and their resources in a way that has never been attempted before. As one BC government official said, "They're warriors out there. They are skilled, and there are two things they have: they work hard and they are as educated as anyone. They understand what is and isn't possible."

> Everybody has evolved. (At the CRB) we talk about the necessity of maintaining the communities, all of the communities. None of us wants to see these communities disappear. First Nations want to use *hahuulhi* as a frame. They talk about the sea, they talk about all resources. It's very much stewardship. It's very much the desire to have the abundance that existed in all those realms. The crux is that everything is so low. We need to build up the stocks and continue on. Local management is the way for here. The trick is getting everyone involved.
>
> —Central Region Board member

What is possible in Clayoquot Sound, first of all, is to re-imagine its borders. A wholesale rethinking of the Sound's administrative and jurisdictional boundaries is required. Clayoquot Sound should be managed on the basis of its marine resources and its watersheds. It should be managed as a whole system, not subject to an overlapping and inconsistent matrix of imposed administrative systems. It must follow the recommendation of the scientific panel that "*Hahuulhi* will be used in determining ecosystem management within traditional boundary lines."[59] Those boundary lines are traditional Nuu-chah-nulth boundaries, and to manage an ecosystem within those boundaries requires the rethinking of existing jurisdictional boundaries and constraints. That means reworking federal, provincial, regional and local arrangements that continue to stifle responsible stewardship and local initiative. In particular, forest tenures that frustrate economic diversity and community stability should be abandoned in favour of better uses for—and protection of—public lands. This does not mean an end to government, but a return to governance that respects the capacity of the ecosystem and the needs of local people.

It is widely recognized that Clayoquot Sound is an area of worldwide ecological significance. The region is eminently qualified for recognition by UNESCO under its Man and the Biosphere program. Attempts on the part of local and regional scientists, conservationists, and policymakers to pursue MAB designation are continuing. A Man and the Biosphere designation (see sidebar, page 77) can provide important resources and perspective for the management of Clayoquot Sound, and for a shift to stewardship of the Sound that reflects the source of its greatest abundance, the sea, and focuses a great deal less on forest management.

After all, the heart of Clayoquot Sound is its waters. The future of Clayoquot Sound must lie in an understanding of its marine resources and their careful stewardship. Management of the forested landscape should take place only in the context of its effects on hydroriparian systems and near-shore marine systems. The vast and infinitely varied ecosystems of the ocean are even less understood than those of the rain forest. The scientific panel has proved beyond doubt the value of comprehensive and independent scientific definition of practices needed to protect vulnerable ecosystems.

There are significant opportunities for ocean-based economic activities in Clayoquot Sound, even after allowing for the crash of its salmon populations. Mariculture—the farming of shellfish such as oysters, scallops and Manila clams—is a developing industry with enormous potential, yet little processing of shellfish takes place locally.

REDRAWING THE BOUNDARIES— NEW ZEALAND'S "CONSENT" MODEL
By Ian Gill

Redrawing the administrative boundaries of Clayoquot Sound is an ambitious goal, but there is at least one precedent for how it might be done. In 1991, New Zealand passed a Resource Management Act. Two years earlier the country had been divided into distinct regional authorities based on 13 major "water catchments." The previous socio-economic jurisdictions were done away with, as were 20 major and often conflicting statutes. "The act calls for a new attitude to law. Instead of prescribing what activities should or should not be allowed, the act places the emphasis on the effect a proposed activity will or might have on the environment." [1]

The act is administered by the Ministry for the Environment, which issues "consents" for development activities if an applicant can demonstrate that the activity meets the act's goal of "managing the use, development and protection of natural and physical resources in a way, or at a rate, which enables people and communities to provide for their social, economic and cultural well being and for their health and safety."

New Zealand's indigenous peoples, the Maoris, "are given much greater recognition than was the case prior to the last decade," says David Clendon of the University of Auckland.[2] New Zealand's Iwi, or tribes, must be consulted before consents are granted. "The concept of kaitiakitanga (stewardship or responsibility for traditional lands, waterways and resources) is embedded in the act." According to Clendon, "the system is new, and has flaws and shortcomings, but is conducive to a much more inclusive, democratic and ecologically rational process of decision making."

The New Zealand example is offered here for two reasons: first, as encouragement that the progressive reforms in Clayoquot Sound, especially to embrace First Nations management principles and concerns, are not being undertaken in isolation; and second, to suggest that if New Zealand can organize its whole country around watersheds, surely in BC we can experiment at the watershed scale of a Clayoquot Sound.

[1] New Zealand Ministry for the Environment website, http:www.mfe.govt.nz/home/htm.

[2] David Clendon, personal communication.

Marine-based tourism is a burgeoning industry that depends on healthy marine systems and forested viewscapes. But will salmon farming—now a significant industry in Clayoquot Sound—do to the seascape what industrial logging has done to the landscape? Is an ecologically sustainable salmon farming industry possible, or even desirable? Or better yet, is there a way to restore wild salmon to their traditional 192¶ abundance?

The suitability of salmon farming as an economic activity is in doubt because of a wide range of unresolved questions about the potential impact of the industry on marine ecosystems. Whatever the future of the industry, it must not be considered as a better alternative to commercial fishing

There is a shift afoot towards stewardship of Clayoquot Sound that reflects the source of its greatest abundance, the ocean.

or as a reason to relax efforts to restore wild salmon and other fish stocks to their traditional abundance. Fisheries are the traditional lifeblood of rural coastal communities and should be central to the future economic prosperity of Clayoquot Sound. For that to occur, two things will be essential: improved knowledge of all the various factors that affect the rise and fall of fish populations, and a management sys-193¶ tem that ensures the conservation of those populations.

The continuing uncertainty about the effect of salmon farms on other marine species and about the habits of wild fish populations is simply one illustration that there is far less understanding of marine than of terrestrial ecosystems. The Scientific Panel on Sustainable Forest Practices demonstrated the imbalance that exists as a result of decades of emphasis on technical expertise in harvesting systems rather than on scientific understanding of ecosystem dynamics. This is even more true of the management of the oceans. Given the importance of the ocean to the Clayoquot Sound economy, and the wide range of potential economic uses, government should consider appointing a marine scientific panel which could play a vital role in providing the understanding needed to conserve marine ecosystems, and could explore the feasibility of new economic activities (the biotechnology industry, for example) that are currently emerging. A marine scientific panel, like its forests predecessor, could also serve as an 194¶ exemplary model for ocean management practices elsewhere on the Pacific coast.

The Scientific Panel on Sustainable Forestry Practices came as an afterthought to the land-use decision when, logically, it should have preceded and informed planning processes. In the case of ocean management, a marine scientific panel should either precede or exist concurrently with the development of a coastal management plan in 195¶ such a matter that the information it provides is available in a timely manner.

Planning in BC has been heavily focused on forest lands for decades. Yet for over two decades, task forces and independent studies have called for the preparation of a coastal management strategy. Such a strategy would bring together all levels of government and coastal communities to identify issues that contribute to conflict and stagnation in the management of coastal resources, and to prepare a policy and practical framework for the resolution of those issues. Responsibility for coastal management is currently divided among more than 30 provincial and federal agencies with frequently conflicting mandates and objectives. The economic strength of the province in future will largely depend on its ability to develop efficient ways of managing coastal resources in a manner that sustains fragile ocean ecosystems. The current morass of conflicting responsibilities and federal-provincial bickering has produced a paralysis that is no longer affordable.

The situation is particularly acute in Clayoquot Sound, where all communities face and depend on the ocean for their economic well-being and their quality of life. The confusion about government mandates, policies and procedures in coastal management has if anything increased in the wake of the land use decision and in the midst of treaty negotiations. Solutions are desperately needed for ongoing issues such as availability of foreshore tenure, conflicts among competing activities such as wilderness tourism and aquaculture, and conflicting and insufficient information about the capacity of marine ecosystems to sustain certain economic activities.

A coastal management strategy could be complemented by the preparation of local management plans to resolve conflicts among different uses and lay a solid foundation for diverse ocean-based economies. Given its history and its diversity of marine activities, Clayoquot Sound provides an ideal setting for the development of a model coastal management plan that would set the example for other communities. The conclusion of the aquaculture review, of tourism inventories and of federal-provincial negotiations about fisheries responsibilities could provide a logical starting point for the contemplation of a coastal management plan for Clayoquot Sound.

The residents of Clayoquot Sound are weary of government processes that they see as having been undermined or dominated by outside interests—processes that came not only with strings attached but with ropes that immobilized them. Nevertheless, with

196¶

197¶

198¶

AN UNLIKELY STRATEGY FOR CONSERVATION: SHORETRUST, THE FIRST ENVIRONMENTAL BANCORPORATION®
By Edward C. Wolf

ShoreTrust

In the early 1990s two organizations—Ecotrust and Shorebank Corporation—developed an uncommon partnership to promote a new kind of coastal enterprise. ShoreTrust aims to profit from natural capital, while seeking to restore it. It seeks to capture value and reinvest it to enrich the common ground of communities and ecosystems along the rain forest coast. Ecotrust, a non-profit conservation-based development organization based in Port-

land, and Shorebank, a federally regulated bank holding company based in Chicago, have spent five years devising a strategy to deliver resources to environmental entrepreneurs in the North American coastal temperate rain forests. This strategy combines conservation and community development banking, and involves the creation of a permanent development institution.

While the ShoreTrust strategy is designed for expansion to the entire coastal temperate rain forest region, the success of the development effort over the long term depends on demonstrated success in the more medium term; a viable strategy requires tight geographic targeting. Thus Shorebank and Ecotrust sought a specific initial geographic target area where the economy and the ecosystem were in distress, but where sufficient natural assets and community support existed to carry forward the conservation-based development effort. After much review, the target area selected was the Willapa Bay watershed and Lower Columbia River region, an area of adjacent river drainages encompassing more than 650,000 hectares in southwest Washington state and northwest Oregon; it is an area about twice the size of Clayoquot Sound. Subsequent expansion will be implemented by selecting additional tightly targeted sites in other parts of the bioregion. Clayoquot Sound could be one such place.

Recognizing the need to revitalize the Willapa Bay economy, Ecotrust and Shorebank began planning a strategy to help spark local investment and initiate a transition in the economic base of the bio-region. To implement the strategy, Ecotrust and Shorebank began drafting a blueprint for the creation of a set of companies, both for-profit and non-profit, that would initiate and sustain comprehensive conservation-based development. The mission of these institutions, now proposed under a local bank holding company and known collectively as ShoreTrust, is to promote conservation-based development in rural communities, reinvigorating the business base to (1) provide income-earning opportunities for low- and moderate-income residents and (2) promote the restoration and conservation of the region's environment.

In 1993, a Shorebank/Ecotrust team completed the first phase of the strategy, which focused on concept development, a survey of entrepreneurial talent in the target area, and market-testing in a broader economic region including the urban centres that held "green" market opportunities. The team's findings demonstrated the market demand for environmentally restorative goods and services, and confirmed that responsible entrepreneurs in Willapa's coastal towns could develop such products profitably when appropriate incentives and services were in place. Conservation-based development begins from the premise that these natural resource businesses can spur an economic and cultural shift toward ecosystem restoration.

Based on lessons learned during this first phase of the project, Shorebank and Ecotrust launched the second phase of the strategy in 1994 by creating ShoreTrust Trading Group (STTG), the first conservation-based development institution. Headquartered in Ilwaco, Washington, STTG is a non-profit

business development organization offering marketing services, technical assistance, and high-risk, non-bank credit to entrepreneurs in the Willapa Bay and Lower Columbia River target area. STTG's primary strategy is to identify new market opportunities for environmentally sensitive products that could be produced by enterprises in the service area. Through these market opportunities, STTG helps local firms expand their business capacities and identifies entrepreneurs who are capable of starting new businesses. Many companies in the service area that respond to new market opportunities require technical assistance in accounting, modernization, marketing, packaging, production, and business management, along with financing to support expanding operations. Accordingly, STTG offers business management, technical assistance, and credit structured to enable the development of local area company capacities.

STTG services and credit products are provided to locally-owned small and emerging businesses, as well as predominantly low- and moderate-income individuals, in and adjacent to the target area. Customers are required to demonstrate a dedication to conservation-based business practices and an inability to access quality financial and business development services elsewhere. As a targeted effort irrevocably tied to local people and a way of life, STTG is closely linked with the Willapa Bay community. All STTG staff reside in the community and are active in civic and community affairs. The marriage of traditional community development practice and conservation-based development requires this commitment to accountability, both in theory and practice.

In November 1995, working with Ecotrust and with the assistance of US Bancorp, Shorebank acquired ShoreTrust Bank, formerly US Bank of Southwest Washington. Since that acquisition Shorebank and Ecotrust have completed a business plan for the proposed new bank holding company and its subsidiary bank, and are addressing other regulatory requirements prior to making the bank fully operational. Once operational, ShoreTrust Bank will engage in conservation-based development lending, aggressively pursuing all viable opportunities that enhance community development and ecosystem integrity. Ecotrust Canada is now working with a team from Ecotrust and Shorebank to explore ways in which ShoreTrust can best be adapted to the needs of communities in British Columbia.

Marine-based tourism is a burgeoning industry that
depends on healthy marine systems and forested
viewscapes.

their lengthy experience in working with one another, and with a common commitment to conservation-based development, Clayoquot Sound residents would be well
placed to participate in the preparation of a coastal management plan that genuinely
accommodates local interests and takes heed of the lessons provided by ill-fated 1995
processes in earlier years.

A variety of emerging and yet to be developed land-based and ocean-based enterprises
holds promise for greater diversification of Clayoquot Sound's economy in the future.
The expansion of the park system leaves the way open for the building and management of hiking trails to meet the growing demand by tourists. Community supported
facilities for light industrial activities such as oyster shucking and the processing of
salal, for which there is constant demand in the floral trade, could be combined with
a training facility for "Clayoquot Sound apprenticeships" in carving, wildcraft, natural history and ethnobotany. A learning centre could provide a forum for music and
the arts, oral history, cultural reconnaissance, political discussion and community
organizing. An outdoor school might provide courses in kayaking, trail-building, diving, climbing and wilderness first aid, among other activities. Wilderness lodges in
remote areas of Clayoquot Sound could provide a base for a wide range of recreational activities. Diversity of economic activity should be accompanied by a diversity
of locations for that activity, so as not to further marginalize First Nations communi- 2005
ties by centralizing economic expansion in Tofino.

Despite the myriad possibilities, local residents find their efforts to capitalize on economic opportunities frustrated by lingering uncertainties and formidable obstacles.
Access to both land and resources is a continuing problem. As described earlier, businesses engaged in the secondary manufacturing of wood products can't get salvage
timber; local shellfish growers can't sell their products locally because no processing
facility exists. Foreshore is unavailable to meet the growing demand for docking facilities in Tofino, and affordable housing and seasonal accommodation for workers is
virtually unavailable. In addition, there is a critical shortage of industrial space for

small-scale manufacturing. Finally, little professional assistance and virtually no information is available locally for economic planning by local governments and 201¶ entrepreneurs.

There is no single answer to these obstacles and frustrations, although clearly where it does not lie is with the BC government's land use decision, which perpetuated the practice of dividing land into areas protected from all development, and areas dedicated to intensive development of a single resource. The demarcation of territory into completely protected areas and intensive development areas is not the only way to ensure the protection of environmental values. True conservation occurs when communities responsibly manage their territory in such a way that development carefully ensures conservation of natural values. Today, local groups who understand this con-202¶ cept are working to put it into practice.

Clayoquot Sound residents are hungry for economic opportunities that build on local character and respect their sense of place, and have already begun to eschew outside intervention in favor of solutions arrived at locally. A void in authority left in the wake of the Clayoquot Sound land use decision has been filled by a burst of smaller groups that have come onto the scene. The West Coast Sustainability Association, the Kennedy Lake Technical Working Group, the West Coast Forestry Society, the Waterfront Market Society, Forest Watch, the Long Beach Model Forest, and the Value Added Wood Manufacturers Association are all examples of groups that are attempting to influence development by energetically producing new ideas and proposals and sharing them with each other and with governments. Even before the 1993 decision, community projects like the Clayoquot Biosphere Project and Management for a Living Hesquiaht Harbour had begun developing 203¶ local solutions to local problems.

Today, community groups remain disillusioned with traditional methods of public involvement in resource management. They are trying to take action but they are still forced to operate in a climate of sectoral entitlement. In the words of one resident, "When people feel vulnerable, when they don't have security, they feel they have to go after everything and they can't back off from anything they have now." What contributes most to that sense of insecurity for Clayoquot Sound residents is being denied the opportunity to craft their own destiny at a time when they are eminently capable of doing so. What is missing is not the entrepreneurial energy, or the desire to understand and manage change, but a mechanism that allows the articulation of an ecosystem-wide community vision, and then gathers the tools to put that vision into 204¶ practice.

The time is ripe to build on management opportunities in the economic development of Clayoquot Sound. The Central Region Board came into being because of pressure exerted by First Nations. By bringing together government with aboriginal and non-aboriginal residents to review a broad range of development proposals, the CRB is a useful first step towards effective comanagement, but one that is currently constrained by its primary focus on forestry, and by limited research resources. The board is compelled to react to plans put before it, and has not yet developed the

A segment of the Wild Side Heritage Trail, Flores Island.

authority or capacity to initiate an ecosystem planning framework for all Clayoquot Sound. What is needed now is the next layer that knits together the vigorous group initiatives currently underway in Clayoquot Sound, and facilitates their authority to ensure that future development respects ecological integrity, is based on diversity of 205¶ use, and reflects residents' values.

Conservation-based development

Ecotrust Canada believes that conservation-based development, like the traditional Nuu-chah-nulth approach to management, holds some clues as to how to integrate the conservation of natural values with the sustainable use of natural resources. Conservation-based development is guided by four cardinal points: understanding, conservation (and restoration), economic development, and policy reform. Each of these points complements the others, and all are vital to ensuring that Clayoquot 206¶ Sound is managed for the perpetuation of abundance in the coming century.

Understanding

Ecosystem-level research, monitoring of ecological and economic trends, inventories, and education are all key to a level of understanding that should inform any decision that has lasting consequences for an ecosystem. In some measure, that role is already being played in Clayoquot Sound by the Clayoquot Biosphere Project. The Biosphere Project's role as an independent scientific investigator could be a vital enabling tool for community decision making. But science is just one part of what is needed. A broader investigative role needs to be undertaken to assess the economic and ecological consequences of development proposals, monitor public opinion, liaise with governments and generate options for responsible economic development. Research and monitor- 207¶ ing are not only essential, they provide lasting local employment.

[60] Clayoquot Sound Central Region Board, Newsletter, Fall 1996.

Community leaders have called for a team approach to future development, and the consolidation of principles that can be applied to any site. The beginning work for the articulation of these principles already exists in two initiatives that have defined common ground among residents: Tofino's Community Values Survey of 1991 and Ucluelet's 1996 Community Vision Statement. A further articulation of community values—and a useful, long-term tool for measuring progress towards retaining those

208¶ values—can be achieved through the use of community indicators (sidebar, page 90).

Conservation

Under the government land use decision of 1993, about one-third of the land in Clayoquot Sound was protected from resource exploitation, with the remainder open to some kind of industrial use. There is a widespread belief in Clayoquot Sound that the 1993 decision fails to adequately protect the Sound's ecosystems. Although it suggested radical changes to forest practices in the sound, the scientific panel was required to leave the 1993 land use decision intact. The land use plan left unprotected three key watersheds in Clayoquot Sound—the Sydney, the Ursus and the Clayoquot River valleys—plus the Upper Bulson valley. Of the 60 primary watersheds larger than 5,000 hectares on the west coast of Vancouver Island, only five are unlogged. Only two of those, the Megin and the Moyeha, are completely protected. The fragmentation by clearcutting of old-growth temperate rain forests has been virtually complete, and the few remaining pristine watersheds deserve protection for both ecological and economic reasons. In light of that, Ecotrust Canada urges the permanent conservation of the remaining pristine watersheds in Clayoquot Sound: the Sydney,

209¶ Ursus, upper Bulson and Clayoquot River valleys.

While it is important to protect certain natural values from development, it should not be assumed that conservation and protection are synonymous. In communities that value the natural wealth of their surroundings, conservation is recognized as an essential consideration in all economic activities, for it is the only sure means of maintaining the natural capital that fuels an economy from one generation to the next. In Clayoquot Sound, where the natural capital—especially in fisheries and forestry—has been severely depleted for several decades, conservation also means

210¶ replenishing that capital by restoring salmon stocks and damaged forest ecosystems.

Economic Development

There is a strong and growing demand for the products and services Clayoquot Sound can provide, and there are products and markets whose potential has not yet been explored. Ecologically sensitive and economically sound businesses have an important place in the new Clayoquot Sound economy. "To achieve long-term economic health, the (Central Region Board) believes that strategies must be developed to assist new and emerging business and employment initiatives for all local communities in ways that do not simply look to replace jobs lost in the forest or fishing industries."[60] Recognition of local communities as "centres of excellence" would provide a means of setting standards for meeting a growing worldwide demand for high-quality timber, seafood, and tourism experiences. Local communities could work to develop innovative methods for selling products "made in Clayoquot Sound." They could collaborate on tapping the huge "green" market for sustainably produced goods and services, such as furniture. This process could be aided by the

HOW WILL WE KNOW WHEN WE GET THERE? FASHIONING NEW INDICATORS OF COMMUNITY WELL-BEING
By Erin Kellogg

Are things getting better or worse in Clayoquot Sound? That depends on who you ask—and what you ask them. Statistics collected by various government ministries may tell one story based on per capita income, number of jobs, volume of timber harvested, percentage of low birthweight babies, number of high school graduates and other measures. But would people living in Clayoquot Sound see themselves in this story?

An article in the *Atlantic Monthly* in October, 1995, "If the GDP is Up, Why is America Down?" wondered why people were feeling so gloomy when by all standard measures the economy appeared to be booming. "Could it be that the nation's economic experts live in a statistical Potemkin village that hides the economy Americans are really experiencing?" the authors asked.[1]

The question can be rephrased in Clayoquot Sound. Does the volume of timber harvested there have any bearing on the profitability of small businesses in the Sound? Does the total number of salmon caught by local fishers in a given year tell us anything about what it cost—in gas, gear, licences, wages—to catch those salmon? Do either of these measures really indicate how the fish and forests—and people—are faring?

The balance sheet we have been using to measure progress and prosperity in Clayoquot Sound, like that used in British Columbia as a whole, and, for that matter, in Canada, has not painted a particularly accurate picture. Clayoquot Sound's natural capital —its clean air, productive soils, pure water, forests and fish—has been left off of the balance sheet. The reliance on quantitative information, particularly dollars and cents, obscures the flourishing barter economy that has always characterized the Sound: a fish for a boat ride, an engine repair job for a fishing net.

How then can the communities of Clayoquot Sound gauge for themselves their own health, wealth and progress? One way is to do the measuring themselves, to create indicators of well-being that are relevant and useful to their communities. Tofino's Community Values Survey is a good first step toward this type of assessment. Other communities have already initiated "community indica-

tor" processes. The Willapa Alliance and Ecotrust published *Willapa Indicators of Sustainable Community* for the Willapa watershed in southwest Washington state. Eleven indicators under the headings of environment, community and economy were selected and presented.

Several elements are common to these efforts: they all recognize that identifying indicators must be an inclusive, bottom-up process that engages the community; they use indicators that are readily available and easily understood; and they emphasize the ties between the health of the environment, the vitality of the local economy, and community well-being.

Should the people of Clayoquot Sound decide to set benchmarks to gauge progress towards their vision for the future of the region, many of the tools are already in place. The Ahousaht, Hesquiaht, and Tla-o-qui-aht are conducting detailed inventories of their traditional territories and the Clayoquot Biosphere Project is gathering baseline information about the natural history of the sound's marine and terrestrial systems. People in Clayoquot Sound consistently express a desire for better information about the region's economy, community and environment for long-range planning.

The authors of the *Atlantic Monthly* article describe a Genuine Progress Indicator (GPI) that could include things such as the household and volunteer economy, erosion of natural capital, and the loss of leisure. "The (Gross Domestic Product) makes no distinction between economic transactions that add to well-being and those which diminish it; and completely ignores the non-monetary contributions of families, communities and the natural environment. As a result, the GDP masks the breakdown of the social structure and natural habitat; and worse, it portrays this breakdown as economic gain." For example, the Exxon Valdez oil spill, which caused billions of dollars in cleanup and damages, resulted in an increase in GDP. No doubt the cleanup of the Nestucca oil spill along the beaches of Clayoquot Sound in 1988 made a "contribution" to the local economy. But by any genuine measure of material and social well-being, an oil spill is clearly detrimental to a coastal community and its ecosystem. How then to measure genuine progress? A modest indicators effort in Clayoquot Sound, one that could move towards a GPI for the region over time, would be a good way to start.

[1] Cobb, Clifford, Ted Halstead, and Jonathan Rowe. "If the GDP is Up, Why is America Down?" *Atlantic Monthly*. October, 1995.

There is an historic opportunity now to re-invent prosperity in the Sound, to craft a future for the people, and for the place, that holds the promise of abiding and enduring prosperity.

establishment of a permanent development institution, which could provide much needed technical and marketing support, and perhaps even non-traditional credit. One example is ShoreTrust Trading Group in Washington State (see sidebar, page 84).

211¶

Policy Reform

As suggested above, fisheries and forest policies in particular need to be reformed if an ecosystem-based approach to stewardship is to succeed in Clayoquot Sound. A Man and Biosphere designation is a first step towards reconfiguring Clayoquot Sound's management regimes. A watershed planning approach based on the model developed in New Zealand could complement a MAB designation. A restructuring of federal, provincial and regional government policies is also required, but the impetus for this is more likely to come from the communities of Clayoquot Sound rather than from politicians or bureaucracies. To foster a more stable and unified framework for seeking policy change, the communities have expressed a need for some forum for public discussion, a way to capture and channel the enormous spirit and energy that resides within the places and people of Clayoquot Sound.

212¶

At this stage in the evolution of the Clayoquot Sound economy, the development of coherent policies for coastal management has become a vital need. A provincial coastal management strategy and a marine scientific panel and coastal management plan for Clayoquot Sound are all essential elements in the development of coastal policy.

213¶

In the practice of conservation-based development, healthy economies and healthy ecosystems are interdependent, and competition among sectors of interest loses intensity as different groups appreciate the mutual advantage of working together to achieve a balance between economic and ecological stability. The merits of this approach were eloquently described by one resident of Clayoquot Sound during the preparation of this report: 214¶

"We hear the phrase 'healthy resources for healthy communities' a lot, but it can also be turned the other way, to 'healthy communities make healthy resources.' If everyone thought about resources in terms of their quality of life, and respected that the quality of life of everyone in the community was equally important, then we would be thinking like a healthy community. The way we've been doing it, with each person focused on their own needs exclusively and from within their own sector of the economy, has only separated us from each other and from what makes healthy resources. We have to get away from that sectoral way of thinking because it has led to the 215¶ destruction of our resources."

The many proposals outlined above—all of which derive from needs expressed by the communities of Clayoquot Sound—lead inexorably to the conclusion that new institutional capacity is needed in Clayoquot Sound. That is not to denigrate the Central Region Board, but rather to recognize that the CRB is itself a part of a transition. Nor is a call for new institutional capacity a slight against the work of numerous groups that have arisen to fill the vacuum left by the failure of government. Rather, it is to suggest that no one institution has yet come forward that can do it all. Perhaps no single institution *can* do it all, but until true decision-making authority is vested in the local communities, it won't all get done. For example, who will ensure the honest implementation of the scientific panel's recommendations for sustainable forestry? Who will press for forest land tenure reform? Who will redefine forest values? Who will coordinate science and education? Who will marshal the resources to complete the protection of the remaining intact watersheds in Clayoquot Sound? Who will develop a marine protected areas strategy? Who will help ecologically responsible businesses get started, lead them to established markets, and create new markets for goods that people are proud to say come from Clayoquot Sound? Who will promote eco-tourism? Who, finally, will help guide the vital transition from a narrow depen- 216¶ dency on timber to an economy that derives from the abundance of the sea?

"There is fatigue and distrust," says one local observer. "Residents of resource-based and remote communities have a fundamental distrust of government process, rooted partially in a frontier ethic and also in the lack of decision-making and implementation on the ground where people can see." To make decisions, and to implement them on the ground (and the water), to see the results—that is the role the communities of Clayoquot Sound, especially First Nations, have long demanded for 217¶ themselves.

Promoting the need for new institutional capacity in Clayoquot Sound does not invite an implosion to the narrowly local. International, national, provincial and regional perspectives have their place in Clayoquot Sound. A solely local perspective and process runs the risk of a new tyranny driven by local stakeholders, and still subject to inordinate influence, as in this warning from Michael McCloskey, chairman of the

61 "The skeptic: Collaboration has its limits," *High Country News,* 13 May, 1996, 7.

Sierra Club in the US: "Industry thinks its odds are better in these forums. It is ready to train its experts in mastering this process. It believes it can dominate them over time and relieve itself of the burden of tough national rules. It has ways to generate pressures 218¶ in communities where it is strong, which it doesn't have at the national level."[61]

But on the path less travelled, industry will have no greater standing than individuals. Without their timber tenures, the forest companies will no longer have an inflated role in decision making in Clayoquot Sound. Likewise, community fisheries will lessen the role of the industrial fishing fleet in the local economy. The path less travelled leads to a new institutional force for change in Clayoquot Sound, giving the communities there more power, not less. It embraces the Nuu-chah-nulth principles of *hishuk ish ts'awalk* and *hahuulhi*. It follows the key principles of conservation-based development. It both captures energy and releases it, guided by the need to conserve resources, but at the same time promote a viable and ecologically responsible economy. There are too few places in the world where we can even attempt to build a new ethic and a new economy that derives from and enriches an ecosystem as diverse as Clayoquot Sound's. On page 8, in our Introduction, we made several recommendations as to how to implement a conservation-based development strategy in Clayoquot Sound. The ultimate decisions as to what to embrace and what to reject rest with the many communities in Clayoquot Sound. There is an historic opportunity now to re-invent prosperity in the Sound, to craft a future for the people, and for the place, that holds the promise of abiding and enduring prosperity. It is time to see 219¶ the ocean through the trees.

Mapping the Scientific Panel's Watershed-Based Recommendations

BY DAVID CARRUTHERS

The scientific panel wanted the flow of forest products from Clayoquot Sound to be dictated by the local environment, instead of being driven by an imposed quota system governed by an annual allowable cut. In order to achieve this, the panel recommended that at the watershed level, maps should be made which designate reserves of sensitive areas where no harvesting should occur. The idea here is that once highly valued and sensitive areas are set aside, cut-block plans can then be developed on what remains.

The analysis involved in such a study is known as constraint mapping. At the BC Conservation Mapping Consortium office in Victoria, Ecotrust Canada conducted a constraint mapping exercise by bringing together a variety of spatial information, filtering out watersheds that have been over-harvested, areas that are environmentally sensitive or highly valued for cultural reasons, and areas that are currently set aside for protection, such as provincial parks. This process followed the principles outlined in the scientific panel's watershed-based recommendations.

The maps created by Ecotrust Canada should be viewed as a progression—a set of filters which build to the final constraints map (Figure 1). By overlaying each constraint, one by one, it is possible to build a composite progression that identifies areas which should be set aside from development. This mapping exercise relied on the scientific panel's own definitions and used as a basis for the analysis many government data sets. The final map takes recommendations from the scientific panel's report and applies them, for the first time, to the land.

The scientific panel adopted an ecosystem based approach to landscape planning. Recognizing that administrative boundaries do not coincide with ecosystem boundaries, the panel recommended that physiographic or ecological land units be used in land-use planning and resource management. With this in mind, four scales of planning were identified: (1) regional; (2) subregional; (3) watershed; and (4) the site-level planning scale.

Regional and subregional plans assist in identifying general use areas, assessing the cumulative distribution of

Figure 1 Constraint mapping of the scientific panel's watershed-based recommendations.

Note that the second set of constraints, for sensitive and highly valued areas, is shown as one layer here for demonstration purposes. In fact, the constraints for sensitive and highly valued areas are arrived at through a series of six maps, i.e. Maps 2-7 in our sequence on pages 38-49.

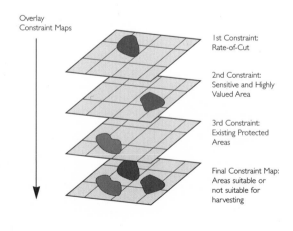

Overlay Constraint Maps

1st Constraint: Rate-of-Cut

2nd Constraint: Sensitive and Highly Valued Area

3rd Constraint: Existing Protected Areas

Final Constraint Map: Areas suitable or not suitable for harvesting

resources and ensuring consistency among lower-level plans. Site-level plans are generally imple-mentation plans, such as studies confirming boundaries of harvestable areas and specific locations acceptable for resource extraction. The panel identified the watershed scale as the basic unit for planning and management in Clayoquot Sound, the scale at which plans are developed to help guide all land-based activities (Figure 2).

At the watershed level, the first constraint to be mapped is the panel's rate-of-cut (ROC) recommendation.[1] The analysis determines if a watershed should be temporarily removed from the forest land base due to past cutting which has extracted too much, too fast. A second series of constraints involves areas that should be removed from the forest land base due to their sensitivity and high biological or cultural values. The third constraint to be mapped is existing protected areas in Clayoquot Sound. Once combined, these three constraints illustrate the total land area where no harvesting should occur, and conversely, areas where sustainable harvesting could take place.

First Constraint:
Rate-of-cut recommendation[2]

The underlying principle in this recommendation is that no more than five per cent of a watershed area should be cut within a five-year period. This applies to watersheds which are larger than 500 hectares. For primary watersheds (watersheds which drain directly into the ocean), the rate is limited to no more than 10 per cent within a 10-year period. Regardless of watershed size, if the rate of cut (ROC) exceeds five per cent in the past five years, but is less than 20 per cent in the past 10 years, a watershed sensitivity analysis and stream channel audit must be completed. In those cases where the ROC exceeds 20 per cent, no further harvesting is permitted until the ROC returns to the acceptable level. Using forest cover information and watershed boundaries, Map 1 illustrates pristine watersheds, watersheds which conform to the ROC, watersheds where a sensitivity analysis and stream channel audit must be completed, and watersheds which should be temporarily removed from the forest base due to cutting which has exceeded 20 per cent of the total watershed area (see also Table 1).

Figure 2 Scientific panel recommended planning hierarchy

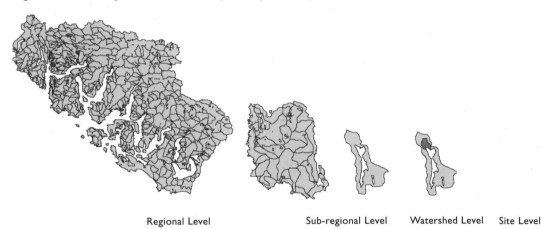

Regional Level Sub-regional Level Watershed Level Site Level

Table 1 Area calculations of watershed status based upon Rate-of-Cut analysis

WATERSHED STATUS	# OF WATERSHEDS	AREA (ha)	% OF TOTAL AREA
Pristine area	219	138 672.38	52.46
Conforms to the ROC	26	16 266.08	6.15
Sensitivity analysis and audit required	67	50 793.48	19.22
Exceeds the ROC– no near-future logging	98	58 613.15	22.17
Total	410	264 345.09	100.00

Note: Total area of Clayoquot Sound = 264 345.09 ha (254 726.04 ha of land; 9 619.05 ha of water)

Second Constraint: Reserves to protect sensitive and highly valued areas

Eight types of reserves were identified by the scientific panel[3] to protect sensitive and highly valued areas. These reserves were recommended to protect: (1) hydroriparian resources (i.e. areas adjacent to water); (2) sensitive soils and unstable terrain; (3) habitat for red- and blue-listed plant and animal species; (4) forest-interior conditions in old-growth forests; (5) important cultural values; (6) areas with high scenic and recreational values; (7) an equal representation of all ecosystems; and (8) links among watershed-level planning areas.

Reserve 1: Hydroriparian resources

Using a complex stream classification system, the panel suggested specific reserve designations for specific hydrological resources. Here, the panel builds on existing recommendations found in the Forest Practices Code and associated guidebooks, such as the *Gully Assessment Procedures for British Columbia Forests*. At the watershed level, streams are classified according to their slope, and given a corresponding reserve buffer size. For example, streams with gradients less than 8 per cent, according to the scientific panel, should be allocated a reserve buffer of 50 metres. Map 2 illustrates these reserves. The panel states that these reserve areas should be excluded from all harvesting activities.

Reserve 2: Sensitive soils and unstable terrain

The panel states that only stable terrain and resilient soils should be made available for forest harvesting operations. Due to the fact that detailed soil maps were unavailable at the time of this study, only slopes were examined in this analysis. Referring to the Forest Practices Code guidebook, *Mapping and Assessing Terrain Stability*, the panel adopted a methodology to determine slope stability at a site-specific scale. Stepping back to the scientific panel's recommended study scale, the watershed unit, the guidebook makes general recommendations that slopes in excess of 60 per cent (31 degrees) are usually too steep for forest activities, and slopes in excess of 70 per cent (35 degrees) are almost certainly too unstable for forest activities (see Figure 3). Using a 3-D elevation model of the Sound, Map 3 illustrates slopes which are steeper than 70 per cent, a conservative approach to determining reserves that will protect potentially unstable terrain.

Reserve 3: Reserves to protect red- and blue-listed plant and animal species

The scientific panel has followed the general shift in conservation management away from a species

Figure 3 Slopes in excess of 70 per cent are generally regarded as areas prone to erosion and thus unsuitable for forest harvesting activities.

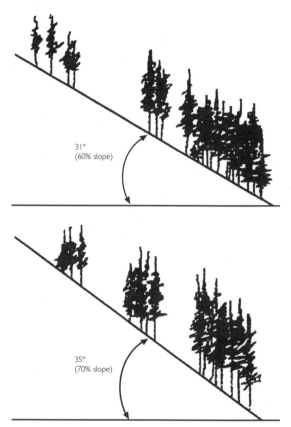

31° (60% slope)

35° (70% slope)

approach to protection, to the preservation of habitats and home ranges of rare or endangered species. The panel recommends that reserves be created for the habitat protection of red- and blue-listed (endangered and threatened) plant and animal species (Table 2). Recognizing that protection is often better implemented at the site-specific scale, and that planning for protection may occur at the subregional scale, maps can be created at the watershed level to help define the boundaries of this reserve designation. Unfortunately, mapping this recommendation is hampered by a lack of habitat information for threatened, endangered, or rare species in Clayoquot Sound. Due to this limitation, this reserve is not included in our set of constraint maps.

Reserve 4: Reserves to protect forest-interior conditions in late successional forests

The scientific panel has recognized that many plants and animals rely on the unique interior conditions of older forests for their survival. The panel stated that, assuming tree heights of 50 m, a reserve width of 300 m will provide at least some forest-interior conditions for these species (Figure 4). Using satellite imagery at a 30 m resolution, older intact forests have been mapped, along with a 300 m interior reserve buffer, and illustrated in Map 4.

The panel notes that the total area reserved in each watershed should not be less than 40 per cent of the total watershed area, and the actual interior area should not be less than 20 per cent of the total area.[5]

Reserve 5: Reserves to protect cultural values
People and local cultures must be considered in any environmental planning exercise. The scientific panel has identified the need to create reserves to protect culturally important areas, including sacred areas, historic sites, and traditional and current use areas. Maps have been created for the provincial archaeology branch to show the extent of known and potential archaeological and current indigenous use areas. These data are illustrated in Map 5. This map is a good starting point in mapping culturally important sites. However, the scientific panel's intent in creating these reserves was to protect only areas identified by the Nuu-chah-nulth First Nations, and thus this map does not include areas of cultural importance to non-aboriginal people living in the Sound. Further

Table 2 Red and Blue listed plant and animal species observed in the Clayoquot Sound area (BCCDB, 1996)[4]

TYPE	SCIENTIFIC NAME	COMMON NAME	RANK
Vascular Plant	Carex pansa	Sand-Dune Sedge	Blue
Vascular Plant	Aster paucicapitatus	Olympic Mountain Aster	Blue
Vascular Plant	Erysimum arenicola var torulosum	Sand-Dwelling Wallflower	Blue
Vascular Plant	Hedysarum occidentale	Western Hedysarum	Blue
Vascular Plant	Epilobium glaberrimum ssp fastigiatum	Smooth Willowherb	Blue
Vascular Plant	Asplenium adulterinum	Corrupt Spleenwort	Blue
Vascular Plant	Romanzoffia tracyi	Tracy's Romanzoffia	Blue
Vascular Plant	Myrica californica	California Wax-Myrtle	Blue
Vascular Plant	Fraxinus latifolia	Oregon Ash	Red
Vascular Plant	Scrophularia lanceolata	Lance-Leaved Figwort	Blue
Vascular Plant	Juncus brevicaudatus	Short-Tailed Rush	Blue
Vascular Plant	Utricularia gibba	Humped Bladderwort	Blue
Vascular Plant	Thelypteris quelpaertensis	Mountain Fern	Blue
Vertebrate	Ptychoramphus aleuticus	Cassin's Auklet	Blue
Vertebrate	Fratercula cirrhata	Tufted Puffin	Blue
Vertebrate	Melanitta perspicillata	Surf Scoter	Blue
Vertebrate	Haliaeetus leucocephalus	Bald Eagle	Blue
Vertebrate	Gulo gulo vancouverensis	Vancouver Island Wolverine	Red

Note: Red = Endangered; Blue = threatened

Figure 4 Buffering old-growth forest to protect forest-interior conditions

 300 m buffer

Forest interior conditions

Old growth forest patches too small to contain interior conditions (i.e. area < 64 ha)

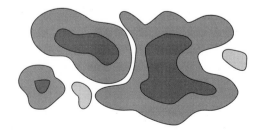

inventories and consultation are required from the Nuu-chah-nulth, and other residents in the Sound.

Reserve 6: Reserves to protect scenic and recreational values

Although difficult to quantify, the panel recommended that areas with high scenic and recreational values should be protected from alteration. The Ministry of Tourism has conducted a detailed scenic corridors analysis of the Sound,[6] complemented by maps of recreational use areas. These maps illustrate highly visible areas which have not been altered, areas visible from communities, important recreational sites, and areas with a strong recreational focus, such as hiking trails and popular kayaking routes. Combined, these areas are presented in Map 6.

Reserve 7: Reserves to protect all ecosystems

The scientific panel recommended that all of the above reserves, combined with existing protected areas, be overlayed onto one map to determine if all ecosystems are being equally protected. This investigation can be carried out by calculating the percentage of each biogeoclimatic site series (or surrogate) classification protected by the reserves. The panel recommended that, where ecosystems are found to be under-represented, reserves should be created to ensure their proportional protection. In order to carry out this analysis, terrestrial ecosystem maps are required, but are unavailable. Due to this limitation this reserve is not include in our constraint mapping analysis.

Reserve 8: Reserves to ensure links among watershed-planning areas

This reserve designation was suggested by the panel to ensure that all of the reserves are adequately linked together to maximize the migration of animals and plants between units, and to provide connectivity for recreational opportunities. The mapping for this reserve has been done by visual inspection of the combined reserve designations and is illustrated in Map 7. Gaps between large reserve areas and between recreational use areas, such as between hiking trails and camping areas, are joined together by the creation of this final reserve designation.

Third Constraint: Existing Protected Areas

The Ministry of Forests has produced a watershed map which defines the boundaries of Clayoquot Sound.[7] The total land area of the Sound, excluding Meares Island and Tofino, is 254,726.04 hectares. Of this total land base, 34.87 per cent (88,821.66 ha) is protected either provincially or federally. Existing protected

areas are illustrated in Map 8, and comprise the third constraint in the scientific panel mapping exercise.

Final Constraints Map

By combining all of the previous eight maps, a final constraints map is made to show all the areas in the Sound where logging should not occur and areas where sustainable forestry, based on the scientific panel's recommendations, can potentially take place (Map 9).

From Map 9, analysis shows that 22,916.31 ha of the Sound is potentially available for the creation of forest development plans (Table 4).

Combined Constraints Map and Pristine Watersheds

As described on pages 33-34, pristine watersheds are inherently important for economic, cultural and environmental reasons. While the scientific panel's recommendations have gained acceptance, one important critique of the panel's work is that it made no specific recommendations regarding pristine areas. There remains a widespread and well justified belief that the remaining untouched watersheds in Clayoquot Sound should be protected from development. Map 10 combines Map 9, the final constraints map, with a further constraint against logging in pristine valleys. Map 9 suggests the amount of land that can actually be logged in the Sound amounts to 22,916.31 hectares. Map 10 shows the location of the 10,784.11 hectares of land available for logging if the pristine watersheds are protected, and the recommendations of the scientific panel are followed across the entire land base of Clayoquot Sound.

Table 3 Landcover distribution, by area

COVER TYPE	AREA (ha)	% COVER
Old Growth	89 307.66	33.78
Broken Canopy Forest	35 397.12	13.39
Muskeg Forest	38 292.36	14.49
Sparsely Forested	20 221.32	7.65
Natural Deciduous Forest	413.36	0.16
Other vegetation	13 228.43	5.00
Bare / Rock / Sand	14 330.88	5.42
Snow	2772.04	1.05
Old growth edge / 2nd growth	2841.19	1.07
Older 2nd growth	442.86	0.17
Younger regeneration	12 393.44	4.69
Logged / Developed	25 085.38	9.49
Water	9619.05	3.64
Total	**264 345.09**	**100.00**

Table 4 Summary table of the constraints to logging by area

MAP NUMBER	CONSTRAINT	AREA (ha)	% OF TOTAL AREA
1	Rate-of-cut (watersheds which exceed the ROC)	58613.15	23.01
2	Reserves to protect hydroriparian resources	51769.73	20.32
3	Reserves to protect sensitive soils and unstable terrain	70488.50	27.67
4	Reserves to protect forest-interior conditions	104155.09	40.89
5	Reserves to protect cultural values	43788.84	17.19
6	Reserves to protect scenic and recreational values	61813.10	24.27
7	Reserves to ensure links among watershed-planning areas	31182.32	12.24
8	Existing protected areas	88821.66	34.87
9	Final constraints map	231809.18	91.00
10	Final constraints map and pristine watersheds	243941.66	95.77

[1] Scientific Panel for Sustainable Forest Practices in Clayoquot Sound, Report 5: Sustainable Ecosystem Management in Clayoquot Sound: Planning and Practices (April 1995), 237, R3.1

[2] Ibid, 237, R3.1

[3] Ibid, 248, R7.16

[4] BC Conservation Data Centre database of rare species and plant communities, 1996

[5] Scientific panel, op. cit., 170.

[6] Clayoquot Landscape Inventory, Phase 2: Final Report. Juan de Fuca Environmental Consultants, Clayoquot Sound Scenic Corridors Planning Process, Ministry of Small Business, Tourism and Culture, 1994 (unpublished).

[7] Clayoquot Sound Watershed Groups, 1:200,000 map. Allan Chapman, Ministry of Forests, Vancouver Forest Region, 1996 (unpublished).

Clayoquot Sound: A Chronology

ca. **11000 BP** Ice covering Vancouver Island retreats from coastline.

ca. **4000 BP** Douglas-fir, Sitka spruce and hemlock forests well established; Nuu-chah-nulth people settled on the west coast of Vancouver Island.

ca. **3500 BP** The shoreline between ocean and forest stabilized; red-cedars widespread.

1778 Captain James Cook sails *HMS Discovery* and *Resolution* into Nootka Sound, north of Hesquiaht Peninsula, and barters with Nuu-chah-nulth for sea-otter pelts.

1788 Captain John Meares establishes a trading post for furs near Opitsaht, on the island later named for him.

1792 Optisaht burned by American traders following a dispute at Fort Protection, on Meares Island.

1820s Sea otters virtually extirpated from BC coast following decades of hunting.

Early 1800s Ahousaht people move from Vargas to Flores Island, after defeating the Otsosaht.

1843 Fort Victoria is established and becomes a destination for Nuu-chah-nulth trading expeditions.

1871 British Columbia enters the Canadian Confederation.

1874 First permanent white community established on Stubbs Island, near the rebuilt village of Optisaht. Norwegian settler Frederic Thornberg takes charge of Clayoquot Station, buying from the Nuu-chah-nulth furs and dogfish oil, used as a lubricant in the lumber industry.

1884 Canadian government declares potlatch a criminal offence.

1908 Canadian government completes the initial laying out of Indian reserves in BC, confining the Nuu-chah-nulth to 150 reserves totalling less than 5,000 hectares. The Nuu-chah-nulth population has by now been decimated by diseases introduced by Europeans.

1942 Japanese residents of Tofino and Ucluelet removed to detention camps, following Japan's entry into the Second World War.

1955 BC government allocates Tree Farm Licence 22 to BC Forest Products.

1959 Completion of forest access road from Port Alberni provides vehicle access to Clayoquot Sound.

1971 Creation of Pacific Rim National Park.

(BP = Before Present)

1980 Fifteen west coast nations replace the name Nootka with Nuu-chah-nulth ("people all along the mountains") to identify their people, and declare sovereign occupancy over tribal territories on the west coast of Vancouver Island. The Canadian government accepts their land claim for negotiation.

1980 MacMillan Bloedel announces its intention to log Meares Island, sparking the formation of the Friends of Clayoquot Sound, an advocacy group dedicated to the preservation of the rain forest.

1984 Tofino residents organize a boat blockade of Meares Island. The Tla-o-qui-aht and Ahousaht Nations declare the island a Tribal Park and a year later obtain a court injunction against logging pending settlement of their treaties.

1988 Thirty-five protesters are arrested following a blockade of a logging road at Sulphur Pass, north of Flores Island.

1989 The Clayoquot Sound Sustainable Development Task Force, set up by the BC government to develop a sustainable development strategy, collapses over disagreement over interim logging and representation at the table.

1990 A study reveals that of 60 primary watersheds larger than 5000 hectares on the west coast of Vancouver Island, only five remain unlogged, including three in Clayoquot Sound.

1991 BC government establishes Clayoquot Sound Sustainable Development Strategy Steering Committee. Environmental representatives walk out following a decision to approve interim logging.

1992 BC government instructs Commission on Resources and Environment to develop a comprehensive land use plan for Vancouver Island, excluding Clayoquot Sound. Sixty-five people are arrested in a blockade at the Clayoquot Arm bridge.

1993 Following the failure of the Steering Committee to reach full agreement on areas to be protected, the BC government announces the Clayoquot Sound land use decision. In protest, the Friends of Clayoquot Sound organize a blockade at Kennedy bridge. More than 800 are arrested. The government appoints the Scientific Panel for Sustainable Forest Practices in Clayoquot Sound.

1994 The BC government and Nuu-chah-nulth Nations negotiate an Interim Measures Agreement providing for joint management of lands and resources in Clayoquot Sound and setting up a Central Region Board to oversee planning and development.

1995 Scientific panel releases detailed recommendations for the implementation of forest management with priority given to ecosystem protection rather than timber production. Cabinet agrees to implement all the panel's recommendations.

1997 MacMillan Bloedel announces that it is shutting its Clayoquot Sound logging operations for at least one year.

Selected Bibliography

Arima, E.Y. *The West Coast (Nootka) People*. British Columbia
Provincial Museum Special Publication No. 6. Victoria, 1983.

Berman, Tzeporah, et al. *Clayoquot & Dissent*. Vancouver: Ronsdale
Press, 1994.

British Columbia Commission on Resources and Environment.
Vancouver Island Land Use Plan. Victoria, 1994.

British Columbia Government. *Clayoquot Sound Land Use Decision:
Background Report*. Victoria, 1993.

British Columbia Ombudsman Office. *Administrative Fairness of the
Process Leading to the Clayoquot Sound Land Use Decision*.
Victoria, 1993.

Darling, Craig. *In Search of Consensus: An Evaluation of the
Clayoquot Sound Sustainable Development Task Force Process*.
Victoria: UVic Institute for Dispute Resolution, 1991.

Drucker, Philip. *Cultures of the North Pacific Coast*. Scranton, Pa.:
Chandler Publishing Co., 1965.

Dorst, Adrian and Cameron Young. *Clayoquot: On the Wild Side*.
Vancouver: Western Canada Wilderness Committee, 1990.

Efrat, Barbara and W.J. Langlois. *Nut.ka. Captain Cook and the
Spanish Explorers on the Coast*. Sound Heritage, vol. VII, no. I.
Victoria: Ministry of Provincial Secretary and Travel Industry,
1978.

———. *Nut.ka. The History and Survival of Nootkan Culture*.
Sound Heritage, vol. VII, no. II. Victoria: Ministry of the
Provincial Secretary and Travel Industry, 1978.

Glavin, Terry. *Dead Reckoning: Confronting the Crisis in Pacific
Fisheries*. Vancouver, Douglas & McIntyre, 1996.

Kellogg, Erin, ed. *The Rain Forests of Home: An Atlas of People and
Place. Part 1: Natural Forests and Native Languages of the Coastal
Temperate Rain Forest*. Portland, Oregon: Ecotrust, Pacific GIS,
Conservation International, 1995.

MacIsaac, Ron and Anne Champagne, eds. *Clayoquot Mass Trials:
Defending the Rainforest*. Philadelphia, Gabriola Island: New
Society Publishers, 1994.

M'Gonigle, Michael and Ben Parfitt. *Forestopia: A Practical Guide to
the New Forest Economy*. Madeira Park, BC: Harbour Publishing,
1994.

Moore, Keith. *Coastal Watersheds: An Inventory of Watersheds in the
Coastal Temperate Forests of British Columbia*. Earthlife Canada
Foundation & Ecotrust/Conservation International, 1991.

Neering, Rosemary. *The Coast of British Columbia*. Vancouver:
Whitecap Books, 1991.

Pinkerton, Evelyn and Martin Weinstein. *Fisheries that Work:
Sustainability Through Community-based Management*.
Vancouver: David Suzuki Foundation, 1995.

Radcliffe, Gillian, ed. *Clayoquot Sound: Life Support Services and
Natural Diversity*. (A report to the Strategy for Sustainable
Development for Clayoquot Sound) Madrone Consultants Ltd.,
1991.

Scientific Panel for Sustainable Forest Practices in Clayoquot
Sound. *Report 1*. Victoria, 1994.

———. *Report 2: Review of Current Forest Practice Standards in
Clayoquot Sound*. Victoria, 1994.

———. *Report 3: First Nations' Perspectives Relating to Forest
Practices Standards in Clayoquot Sound*. Victoria, 1995.

———. *Report 4: A Vision and Its Context: Global Context for
Forest Practices in Clayoquot Sound*. Victoria, 1995.

———. *Report 5: Sustainable Ecosystem Management in Clayoquot
Sound*. Victoria, 1995.

Thomson, Richard. *Oceanography of the British Columbia Coast*.
Ottawa: Department of Fisheries and Oceans, 1981.

Young, Cameron. *The Forests of British Columbia*. Vancouver:
Whitecap Books, 1985.

Contributors

Edward H. Backus is president and co-founder of Interrain Pacific, headquartered in Portland, Oregon. He is a co-founder of the BC Conservation Mapping Consortium and initiated the GIS training partnership in the village of Ahousaht, in Clayoquot Sound. For seven years Edward was co-director of the conservation planning group at Conservation International, working throughout Latin America and based in Washington, DC. He has held similar positions with The Nature Conservancy's international program, the US Agency for International Development (Rwanda), and the Puerto Rico Department of Natural Resources. Edward has a BS in wildlife biology from the University of Vermont, and an MFS in resource information management from the Yale University School of Forestry and Environmental Studies.

Spencer B. Beebe is founder and president of Ecotrust in Portland, Oregon. He served in the Peace Corps in Honduras from 1968-71 and after 14 years with The Nature Conservancy as Northwest representative, western regional director, vice-president and president of the conservancy's international program, was the founding president of Conservation International in 1987. Spencer founded Ecotrust in February 1991. In addition to his work with Ecotrust, Spencer serves on the boards of a variety of national and international conservation organizations. He earned his MFS (Forest Science) in 1974 from Yale University's School of Forestry and Environmental Studies, and a BA in Economics from Williams College in 1968.

David A. Carruthers, Director of Information Systems for Ecotrust Canada, has a MS degree in resource management from the University of Edinburgh, where he was invited to research the habitat distribution of bighorn sheep in Wyoming. David has consulted in GIS and spatial analysis for Parks Canada, State of the Environment Reporting, American Wildlands, Ducks Unlimited and other public and private environmental organizations. He has complemented his practical work

experience with teaching experience in GIS and statistics at the University of Edinburgh. He currently manages the BC Conservation Mapping Consortium.

Dan Edwards is a director of the West Coast Sustainability Association and a former self-employed fisher who lives in Ucluelet. Dan has also worked as a forestry engineer with MacMillan Bloedel. He is a co-founder of the Thornton Creek Enhancement Society, and holds a number of volunteer positions with community organizations concerned with coastal fisheries and forestry issues.

Roman Frank has lived almost his entire life in Ahousaht, where he has learned his most important lessons from many elders, his parents, grandparents, and other relatives who have offered him great support. He began work in the Ahousaht GIS (Geographic Information Systems) department in March 1995, along with Tom Paul. Roman and Tom are now members of the community GIS team at the Long Beach Model Forest. Roman is also a member of the board of directors of the Clayoquot Biosphere Project, and is working with others to help to set protocols for research within Clayoquot Sound.

Ian Gill is the founding executive director of Ecotrust Canada. Prior to joining Ecotrust Canada, Ian was a writer-broadcaster with the Canadian Broadcasting Corporation, specializing in land-use, environment and resource issues. His television documentaries won numerous local and international awards. Ian also spent seven years as a senior reporter and editor with The Vancouver Sun. He is a fellow of Journalistes en Europe (1986-87), and contributes frequent articles and commentary to magazines, newspapers, television and radio programs. Ian is a director of the Clayoquot Biosphere Project, and the Nanakila Institute. He is a member of the advisory board of the Cascadia Times newspaper, and of the Forestry Advisory Council at the University of BC. Ian is also a vice-president of Ecotrust, based in Portland, Oregon. He is the author of *Hiking on the Edge:*

Canada's West Coast Trail, and the forthcoming *Haida Gwaii: Journeys Through the Queen Charlotte Islands.*

David Greer is a former Associate with the BC Commission on Resources and Environment, prior to which he spent eight years with the BC and Alberta Ombudsman offices resolving natural resource management disputes. He is the author of *Simple Pleasures* and *White Horses and Shooting Stars.*

Erin Kellogg, Director of Policy at Ecotrust, is a 1991 Master's graduate from Yale's School of Forestry and Environmental Studies. She also earned her BA from Yale College in Russian and Eastern European Studies. Before moving to Portland, Oregon, she worked for a number of government and nonprofit organizations, focusing on environmental policy and sustainability. Erin coordinates Ecotrust's programs in public policy, where most of her work centres on finding ways to translate lessons learned at the community level into recommendations for policy reform. She currently co-chairs the board of The Food Alliance and has served on the board of the Prince William Sound Science Centre in Cordova, Alaska since 1995.

Katrina Kucey, Director of Community Programs for Ecotrust Canada, has a MS degree in rural planning and development from the University of Guelph, which she used as a vehicle to gain professional insight into the areas of community-based forestry and economic development. Since 1988 Katrina has worked in a professional and research capacity with over 40 communities, identifying opportunities in strategic planning and community development. This work has allowed her to live in and develop an intimate knowledge of development issues in areas as diverse as BC's Chilcotin region, northern Manitoba, Clayoquot Sound, southern Ontario, Trinidad, Tanzania and the Philippines.

Lisa Lackey, senior GIS analyst with Interrain Pacific, is an expert in satellite image analysis and landscape cumulative effects of forest management. She is a former manager of the GIS laboratory for the Portland office of Pacific Meridian, a large natural resource consulting firm working on assessment for the USDA Forest Service. Lisa has an MS in integrated pest management from University of California-Riverside and a BA from Southern Oregon State University.

Michael Mertens is a GIS analyst with Interrain Pacific, Portland, Oregon. Mike has a BS in resource management from Humboldt State University. He has worked in county and watershed planning in northern California. Mike has done intertidal resources analysis in the Willapa Bay ecosystem in Washington state, and was principal analyst for the *Kowesas Watershed Assessment* in the Kitlope ecosystem.

Umeek, also known as Richard Atleo, is an instructor in First Nations studies at Malaspina University-College on Vancouver Island. He is a hereditary chief of the Ahousaht First Nation, and was co-chair of the Clayoquot Sound Scientific Panel for Sustainable Forest Practices in 1993-95. Umeek has had a long career in education and anthropology, and has worked for both the Canadian and BC governments. He has had numerous community appointments, and currently is a director of Umeek Human Resource Development Inc. He has PhD and Master's degrees in education.

Edward C. Wolf is Director of Communications at Ecotrust in Portland, Oregon. He holds a Master's degree from the College of Forest Resources at the University of Washington, and has profiled innovative conservation efforts in southern Africa, Latin America, and the coastal temperate rain forests of North America for a number of publications and non-profit organizations.

Ecotrust Canada

Ecotrust Canada is a private, non-profit organization developing creative and innovative approaches to conservation-based development in the coastal temperate rain forests of British Columbia.

Ecotrust Canada works with local communities, First Nations, all levels of government, scientists, industry and fellow conservationists. We are agents of change, catalysts in the ongoing search for true sustainable development of British Columbia's unmatched natural resources.

While not a membership organization, Ecotrust Canada welcomes the support of all who would like to share in our work.

**CONTRIBUTIONS TO ECOTRUST CANADA
ARE TAX DEDUCTIBLE**

Ecotrust Canada
420-1122 Mainland Street
Vancouver, BC
V6B 5L1
Tel (604) 682-4141
Fax (604) 682-1944

Project Office
115 First Avenue West
Prince Rupert, BC
V8J 4K1
Tel (250) 627-7798
Fax (250) 627-8493

Mapping Consortium
1216 Broad Street
Second Floor
Victoria, BC
V8W 2A5
Tel (250) 480-1854
Fax (250) 480-1375

e-mail: info@ecotrustcan.org
katrinak@ecotrustcan.org
dcarruthers@pacificcoast.net

www.ecotrust.org/etcan.htm